David Bleathman
Gordon House
The Street
Boscgrave

THE IMPOSSIBLE THEATRE

The Impossible Theatre

The Chichester Festival Theatre Adventure

Leslie Evershed-Martin

With a Prologue
by
Laurence Olivier

Phillimore
London and Chichester

1971
Published by
PHILLIMORE & CO. LTD.
Shopwyke Hall, Chichester, Sussex

Text © Leslie Evershed-Martin 1971
Prologue © Laurence Olivier 1971

SBN 900592 17 6

Set in 'Monotype' Caslon Series 128 and printed by Gordon Norwood
at the Roundwood Press, Kineton, in the County of Warwick,
on Antique Laid paper. Lithography by Avon Litho Ltd., Stratford-upon-Avon
Made and Printed in Great Britain

Contents

Acknowledgments

I am grateful to Sir Laurence Olivier for his generous Prologue, to The Lord Bishop of Chichester for his sermon, to Sir Tyrone Guthrie for extracts from his Chichester lectures and to Mr Christopher Fry for his two Odes.

I also want to thank Mr Derek Jewell, Mr Francis Steer, Mr Sam Lyons and Mr David Goodman for their guidance and help. I am indebted to the BBC for several quotations from the text of their film 'The Concrete Vision' and to the *Daily Telegraph* for the use of their article 'The Impossible Theatre' by T. S. Ferguson.

Prologue

MY WIFE JOAN and I were lying out on the grass outside the back of the theatre between the last matinee and the last evening show of the first season at Chichester in 1962. A few other members of the company were scattered around, munching their sandwiches or not as the case might be. There were also a hundred or so members of the public scattered at distances between ten and twenty yards from each other. The atmosphere was peaceful. I suppose we all felt rather like sheep — rather like sheep feel, I mean — either eating or not, looking at the grass or beyond it to that lovely group of maples halfway up Oaklands Park. There was very little conversation : there was indeed very little to say.

There was one thought that Joan and I shared and it was a thought that brought more satisfaction than either of us had known for the last six months or so, since our eldest son was born that is to say. 'Well, we've done it, after all; after all that, after all those terrors it finally seems to turn out that we have done it, that we have launched the theatre, that it can open again next year, and that the season has not been a fiasco, and that the Chichester Festival Theatre will not go down to history as the theatre that was once open for ten weeks.'

Lying on the grass beside Joanie at this time before the last performance of our one unquestioned success, which was *Uncle Vanya*, my mind went back as it had so often done to the first sentence of the first brochure that Leslie Evershed-Martin ever sent out, one of which was sent to me—not with any purpose, I think, beyond my interest as a member of the public and as a fairly prominent member of my profession. I always remember the phrase, it seemed so quaint and Jane Austenlike in its genteel assertion —

'A theatre is to be built in Chichester . . .'

It used to go round my head in various forms —

A theatre is in Chichester to be built.

There is to be built in Chichester a theatre.

There is in Chichester a theatre to be built.

and so on.

It is a wee bit curious to recollect that possibly my first feeling of warmth may have been dictated by the fact that the Cathedral at Chichester was the only one that could be found in the country with a set of bells which were of the type congruent with the period of Richard III, for the coronation scene of which film the Dean of Chichester most kindly gave me permission to photograph them.

A little while after I first received this first brochure I had a call from Tyrone Guthrie saying that perhaps I might like to help him do something about it, just as an opener, so to speak — Oh. . . a Shakespeare and a Shaw for three or four weeks, and did I think I might find time for this. Nothing more happened beyond this. As the theatre had not started to be built yet, and as far as anybody could judge did not even look like starting to be built, there really was not any great significance about my either accepting or declining Guthrie's suggestion, so we chuckled a bit over one or two other things and put down our respective phones.

That must have been some time in 1960, since the original idea had hit Evershed-Martin on January 4, 1959 while watching his 'telly'.

The next I heard of it I was in New York, playing in Anouilh's *Becket*. Joan was also there playing in *A Taste of Honey*. I received a letter from Evershed-Martin, which had been written on January 11, 1961. There was something about the offer that caught my fancy, enough at least to think and talk about it, and think and talk about it more and more frequently as the days and weeks went by.

It was a good time to take a long steady look at my life. I had recently had two theatres seemingly pulled down about my ears, the St. James's, in the eight years running of which I had squandered all but my entire resources, and a little later the Stoll, which saw its last performance in *Titus Andronicus*, and I began to think that my presence in a London theatre would only be enviable to a member of the I.R.A.

Also I had lately, after spending nine months going round quite a bit of the world with my hat in my hand, failed to raise the money for what was to have been my fourth Shakespeare film, *Macbeth*. Korda had died, the new 7 % Bank Rate had frightened off the Rank Group, and I was no Mike Todd in the selling of my own wares and I thought I perceived certain writing upon the wall of an unwelcome kind, and decided it was time to put paid to that merry and highly enjoyable little side to my career.

This new theatre, affording new shape (for the last 400 years anyway), new ideas, new functions, new thinking just at this moment in time seemed to me just exactly what the dear, kind doctor had ordered. Apart from creating my own films I had known no joy in all my life's work equal to that of forming a new theatre group.

Consequently, by January 25, I was feeling the need for the Chichester idea to be examined at closer quarters than was possible from where I was, by my close friend and manager of long standing, Cecil Tennant, so on that date I wrote to Evershed-Martin asking him to talk to him and tell him all about it.

There were two or three more exchanges during which I made some stipulations about the working side of the theatre — switchboard, entrance arrangements, etc. I found it difficult to feel altogether comfy about the almost aggressive cleanness of the hexagonal shape of the theatre which seemed to suggest rather a clinical attitude with its broad, arrowhead statement of a stage.

Also, it seemed that the architects had fixed in their minds that the dynamics of such a theatre necessitated that there seemed to be no backstage area at all, and that all the action should flow back and forth through the audience. I suspect that it was the Assembly Hall at Edinburgh that gave them this idea, but it worried me that Juliet should always have to make her entrance through the audience, drop them a little bob, and mount up the staircase and settle herself there waiting until Romeo arrived, Juliet having either pulled the staircase up after her or the audience caused to pretend either that that it did not exist or that Romeo did not see it, or that he was too modest a character as to be so forward as to use it. I also explained the fact that Shakespeare himself most certainly had entrances from backstage and there is never any indication of actors marching through the audience to ascend to it, and they would without doubt have been subjected to some unwelcome horseplay from the groundlings if they had tried. There were a number of other technical points.

Finally I accepted the job on March 3, 1961.

We returned on the *Queen Elizabeth* in June to an unusually avidly interested press. By this time Joanie was what is called 'proud' with our first infant and we both felt concerned by the influx of journalists who took the trouble to embark at Le Havre where the Q.E. called before docking at Southampton, all of them anxious for only one thing — a photograph of 'that bulge'. Both Joanie and I had a natural revulsion from the idea of having that bulge photographed for such widespread distribution and set our hearts, and our faces too, against it.

By some incredible legerdemain Cecil Tennant managed to get Joanie off the boat without being noticed and I stayed behind to draw off the pursuit. This was hot and strong and did not relax for three weeks, and it was that amount of time before we felt inclined to venture out to have a look at Chichester. Even so, we were followed by a car we knew well by this time, which miraculously ran out of petrol before we were halfway there.

We were late for Evershed-Martin and made an extremely apologetic entry into his establishment. He greeted us with breezy efficiency, not looking at either of us very much; shyness one wondered, genuine lack of interest, a wish to seem not overconcerned; or put out because of our unpunctuality; the bonhomie soon dispelled this last, and of other possibilities we thought time would tell. (Please note: my psychology is merely that of an interpretive craftsman and lays no claim to any scientific foundation whatever). He seemed intent in every action to give the impression that he knew what he was about. If he shot a question you felt it was a testing one rather than a wish for information. His face, largish, longish, displayed a pleasantly open countenance, a good, formidable, interestingly sculptured nose, thin lips, large strong teeth, an ever rebellious tuft at the back of his strongly growing pale grey hair, and the skin of his eyelids pulled down at the outer corners a bit, producing a slightly sly expression. At board meetings later I thought it to be part of his public mask deemed to produce an effect of shrewdness.

I have noted from time to time the many and various masks or make-ups that people use, either consciously or unconsciously. Mr Ben Chifley, M.P., of Australia had the most obvious example I have ever known of the politician's hooded eye, the real shutter of the eye's expression, disguising entirely whether he believed or not in the truth of what he was saying, and able at any time to pretend that he was deaf. With Mr Chifley this make-up was pretty well a permanency, at least I never saw him drop it. With Mr Wilson it switched on and off with an almost cynical deliberation. This is not to decry Mr Wilson. It is part of the realistic attitude towards his work which I personally have always found most commendable. In Churchill I never saw it once. His eye was alert and ever bright with interest as if genuinely fascinated to know your opinion of a quite casual remark. If Leslie Evershed-Martin had faults I never discerned them to be more gross than the minor ones universally attached to those of Aldermanic standing. The attitude of those conscious of a slightly elevated position to their fellow townsfolk and a little consciously superior in usefulness.

We went straight to the site and it was a mass of flat mud, and sticking up in it were six drainpipe-like objects about eight feet high, marking out the central shape of the theatre and the positions that the six main supports of it were to take.

We met his wife Carol, a comely, charming, blessed woman and friend, and his two extremely nice, though equally extremely unlike, sons David and Barry.

The idea of opening a theatre in well under a year from the time at which its only manifestation was six drainpipes, seemed to offer to me more of a challenge than is usually associated with that well worn word. However, we were well and truly stuck with it by now and a series of board meetings, with Leslie in the Chair, started.

Joanie and I stayed at the *Royal Crescent* Hotel for the six months that it took for our house in the Crescent to be made ready for us. Apart from the planning and the decorating of the house there was little to occupy me except for plans for Chichester, apart from one job I had which only took about a week, I think, which was to make records of a major portion of the Old Testament.

Our boy was born on December 3, and almost immediately after this I went across to Ireland to make a picture with Simone Signoret, and a new little girl called Sarah Miles, directed by Peter Glenville, called *Term of Trial*. After six weeks, Joan and little Dickie came over and I began to have people from the Chichester enterprise come to visit me in Ireland — Sean Kenny, Roger Furse, Pieter Rogers (the General Manager) etc.

It is always nice if you are making a film to have some stage production to be thinking of, that is if you are merely acting in a film and providing of course that you have taken the precaution of learning your part before you start, and so this was a wonderfully happy time for me.

I suppose it was not unnatural that people regarded my choice of plays as being not general enough. I think that critical and public taste would have been better pleased with a more obvious one-Shakespeare-one-Restoration-and-one-Shaw, even if the obviousness of such a choice may well have struck them as being a little unadventurous.

The reasons for my choice of plays, which were *The Chances*, a Beaumont and Fletcher re-written by the Duke of Buckingham, *The Broken Heart* by Ford, and *Uncle Vanya* by Chekhov, were that these three plays offered me three entirely different styles with which to show off the amenities of this particular theatre : the first with no sets at all beyond that designed more or less for permanency by the architect ; the second as scenically ambitious as it could well be without impinging upon the lines of sight ; and the third utterly realistic.

This is how I saw it at first. It was only after a long day with Sean Kenny on *Uncle Vanya* that I changed my ideas on the realistic approach to *Uncle Vanya*

I felt that my first job was to test the theatre out for the edification of other directors as much as for anybody else. The Chekhov being the most realistic and obviously being supposed to be the least likely to succeed on such a stage as this, ostensibly and traditionally requiring all the realism that a picture stage could afford,

From the portrait of Sir Laurence Olivier, painted in 1968 by Bernard Hailstone.
In the Author's possession.

both Sean and I thought would be interesting only if we adopted a completely different attitude towards it. Therefore, no real birch trees in the garden.

No first snow falling round a little realistic study snugly set in the upper stage, but a set that never changed at all, and very late one night one of those blessed ideas came to me while we were talking and that was to have two windows with black behind them for the outdoor scene, and by simply blacking out on the garden and bringing moonlight up from the other side of these same two windows, the same set, without moving a stick of furniture, changed from an exterior to an interior in as many seconds as one wanted to take over the lighting cue.

It was the actors, by their *behaviour*, Sean and I maintained, from whom the audience should tell whether they were outside the house or inside it, and what sort of a room they were in — a drawing room or an estate office. With this particular discipline of *Chairs* being *any* sort of chairs, of *The* Table being *a* table, one's pride would not admit the idea of black-coated figures coming on and fussing around the set in the intervals. My joyful realization can well be imagined while re-reading the play with these plans in mind when, early on in the second act, I came upon the Nurse saying 'Why, the samovar has not been cleared yet' (the samovar as it happens having been left on from its place on the table in the garden in the previous scene).

Later we found ways close to the beginning of any of the last three scenes — Sybil Thorndike as the Nurse and Lewis Casson as Telyegin casually changing the tablecloth, thereby almost imperceptibly, and with such simplicity that you would hardly think it had meant anything, but somehow or other it did quite definitely become a different room. I have never consciously been given such a bright gift of solution as that line of Sybil's about the samovar early in Act 2, since Ophelia's rosemary on the arm of Hamlet's chair in the film many years before, or the Globe Playhouse frame in *Henry V*, even before that. I am sorry if this seems as if I am blowing my own trumpet but I always think one should recognize little things like this and be thankful for them.

We opened, as Evershed-Martin will tell you, with *The Chances*. At the outset please let me say that I am not over-fond of the idea of actors entering through the audience. I have a feeling that audiences don't like it much — in fact I don't like it much myself. It either pre-supposes that the audience is not there, and no audience can possibly be expected to believe that, or 'we are altogether chums in the same boat really and isn't it all fun' which I myself feel an equal revulsion against, but there you are, this was one of the main ploys in this new theatre and I thought I had best play around with it.

In *The Chances* I thought I did explore every conceivable aspect of this idea once and for all and get it done with. I was in fact starting life in this theatre almost by sending it up. This conception was, I am afraid, misread, and to at least half of our critics the production was either fussy or self-conscious. One thing I did realize, and that was that the first play that anybody saw in this theatre would have very little chance against its greatest rival, namely its home, the theatre itself, and that the bulk of the audience and the critics' attention would be taken up with the theatre rather than what was going on upon the stage. For that reason I did not want deliberately to spoil the chance of an outstandingly noble piece of work.

The Chances was a romp and to my mind still a very endearing and pleasant little romp, but I knew its chances were slender and so, as it turned out, was its portion, though I still quite frequently come across those who, after the initial preoccupation with the theatre itself, enjoyed the piece and the show for its own sake.

Not so, I am afraid, Ford's *The Broken Heart*. This is, and would always be at the very best of times, a difficult piece and I freely admit that I was trying to be too clever and over-anxious in not wishing to be thought afraid to be recondite. It was quite a dreadful flop, and though I felt betrayed by the senior critic who had in the first instance suggested the play to me, and when he came to review it not only condemned the play and the performance but by a wickedly brilliant parody typifying the play's style of dialogue had the gall to condemn even the choice itself, when I would have been as ignorant of the play's existence as well as anybody else, had he not suggested it. (I have had it out with him since, of course, but he honestly doesn't remember suggesting it, he says. I have been quoted as saying 'There is only one way to treat a critic — hit him'. There is something in it).

The Broken Heart I think never played to more than 50% business and though the title proved to be all too prophetic I still think it was worth doing. It is a very strange piece of work with a very odd moral attitude. Its theme is, roughly, Spartan behaviourism. There is a cute story (not in the play) that the Macedonians or the Thessalonians or the Athenians or one of the others of them, once sent a message to Sparta otherwise called Laconia to this effect: 'If you do not instantly yield your so-and-so and pay us so-and-so-and-so, we shall descend upon you with fire and sword and extinguish your race', and the laconic message came back: 'If'. Anyway, self-punishment obviously fascinated John Ford but I think it unlikely that he was a Cicestrian.

Well, there we were, two flops on our hands, though the Box Office for *The Chances* was quite merry, it was playing a slow march for *The Broken Heart*. Critically we were a disaster, both for the first two productions and for the theatre itself. I was not particularly disturbed about the attitude taken regarding the theatre — not because I cared more for my own skin than Evershed-Martin's, but because I knew, should the theatre survive, that in England it would not be long before people got used to it, and not only think that it was quite all right but in time that it was absolutely spiffing.

My chief concern was in making such a crashing flop of the first season with such a uniquely illustrious company as I was lucky enough to have with me, that I would sink the ship while its crew would probably manage to come up for air after a time.

So here we were faced with the last and least likely to succeed of all three productions. They were written in neon lights across my brain, all and every night, my anticipated quotes from the press — 'Of all idiotic choices for this place', 'Could there be chosen a play less likely to succeed', etc. etc.

I forgot to mention that one of the worst luck cards that turned up was — not by design, I firmly believe, but by a leak — the disclosure in the press that I was to direct the future National Theatre; that I am sure (though without particular malice aforethought) added to the weight of the bullets which came our way.

I have never before in my life faced a first night with more certainty of failure than I did that of our third offering — *Uncle Vanya* At the final dress rehearsal everything that could conceivably go wrong, went wrong. It was very hard indeed for this small cast, old stagers though most of us were, to rise above the sense of panic that was everywhere only just under the surface. We all realized, I think, the thinness of the ice upon which we trod when we realized that our fate, or a large share of it, lay in the hands of a young girl who was not really as experienced as she might have been, who was in charge of the tape machine. In the final run through when there should have been a peal of thunder, a guitar played, and when the guitar should have played, a dog barked, etc. etc.

I did not realize how ill this was making Joanie until the end of the performance, during the last act of which she had imagined she heard people hissing and, very unlike Joan indeed, in her dressing room at the end of the evening she had a worrying weeping fit, particularly worrying, of course, since our daughter was upon her way, beneath 'Sonya's' all too tightly laced stays.

Well, Fate flipped the coin to the other side and smiled upon us, but the strain had taken its toll and as Leslie will tell you in a few chapters or so, at the end of our proud Royal evening we had the only bitter row we ever had, for which I take entire blame. When I say that, I mean the conduct and type of row is what I am to blame for, the reason for it is another matter. I felt it would be snapping my fingers in the face of the public to give a presentation of such huge demand as *Uncle Vanya* turned out to be, for 29 performances only. I also felt from Chichester's point of view it would be improvident to bear the costs of a third production the following season, rather than enjoy guaranteed full houses for at least one offering, with no production costs at all. After Chichester's second season it became the third play to be presented at the Old Vic for the National, where it ran in repertory for the whole of the first season. I think it could be running still if circumstances had not forced our company to divide itself into different directions and spheres.

There are two other little points brought to light by this first season at Chichester that might possibly be of interest. The first may seem a suspicion metaphysical but it was felt by all concerned. The theatre had an *entirely* different feeling when one came into it the day after it had for the first time been filled with people, than it had felt the day and all the rehearsal time before this happened. We all remarked upon it. It was there all right and as strong as could be. The difference in atmosphere between an empty just-finished building and forever after the first time it has been filled with an attendant host of people is more remarkable than I, or any of us, ever imagined it could be.

The other difference was the change in atmosphere of the place and its public in the second season from that of the first. The audience had almost stopped entirely looking at the playhouse and were now looking at the play. The jaunty helpfulness of those already initiated to first-comers during the second season was well and truly there.

A little more about Leslie now. There is no question at all but that in getting this theatre built he performed a miracle. As is very natural to a person who does a thing like that he does not appreciate that one miracle in a lifetime is only allowed one person in several generations. He is therefore obliged almost to think of himself as a cat with nine miracles, or even more. Worse than this, it seems to him odd that everybody else has not the same miracle performing gift. His success as a miracle worker not unnaturally, in fact it would be almost inhuman were it not so, influences his characteristics with a certain smugness. This is naturally accompanied by a proneness to be high-handed.

I am sure that he has a reputation for being most awkwardly stubborn. I do not personally blame him for this one iota. It is the prerogative, almost the right, of the person who really believes he is in the right, to be stubborn and I have never blamed him for this. I have in fact never blamed him for anything at all. I think he is a rare specimen in these days, namely a really good man. His worship of tradition, Crichton-like respect of place, utter admission of authority, wanting to do good even if it is in a formalized, institutionalized manner, add up to being virtuous, old-fashioned, I suppose, out of fashion certainly, but virtuous for all that, impossible as such terms may sound to the modern ear without pejorative overtones. They are not qualities which make for high popularity in smallish cathedral towns where admiration for leadership is grudging, contention unashamedly laced with envy, and partiality turns with the speed of onlookers' heads at Wimbledon.

He was the only Mayor of Chichester who got the Sovereign to pay it a visit in 50 years. He is the only man who has caused a theatre to be built in the south of England (apart from replacements obligated by office building laws) for some 30 years, and the first and only man to do it by public subscription in which he alone was the instigator, if not quite alone the go-getter.

If he is high-handed, he is after all a conqueror. If he is self-important, he is in fact really important. If he is self-righteous, he is in truth righteous.

Going back to that feeling which Joan and I shared lying on the grass on the last evening of the '62 season, Leslie Evershed-Martin's account of what led up to this moment frankly makes our efforts pale by comparison. I dare say that the standard of my noble, illustrious actor companions during this season set firm the idea that the Chichester Festival Theatre meant business in that it could not be written off in the usual terms of sincere effort and earnest endeavour usually associated with such beginnings.

I suppose we first lot could claim that we did put it on the map and though the success of the work was by no means entire, rather the reverse, the formidability and quality of the company whose interest we were so fortunate to have, does make its charting more definitive than it would otherwise have been.

The next three seasons were run by the National Theatre and composed of its players. The four years that I was in charge of the Festival it seems that I always would insist on making one mistake out of three. I *would* try to be too clever and the result was in each season one disappointment to the box office.

John Clements who has run the place since 1966 has not made this mistake. This is not to say he has been unadventurous, it is merely to say that he has been more *shrewdly* adventurous than I. Our advance booking for the first season was a little over £30,000. We never achieved anything very spectacularly much larger than this. Last year, the fifth under John Clements' direction, the advance booking reached £140,000. He has more than doubled the interest in the place and under his management it has become a recognized part of English summer life. So to put it very simply, I started it off, John Clements made it good, future directors may swing its fortunes this way or that, but the credit for the fact that the place exists at all will always belong to the man who wrote the book that follows.

LAURENCE OLIVIER

Chapter One

WHO'S FOR SNAKES AND LADDERS?

I have lived
To see inherited my very wishes
And the buildings of my fancy.
                    Shakespeare, *Coriolanus*, Act i i Sc i.

YOU CAN SEE this building on your left as you approach Chichester, the county town of West Sussex, on the A286 road from Midhurst. Set in a park within a horse-shoe of mature elm trees, it is a brown and white concrete hexagon on stilts, with a half-hidden roof pointed like the big top of a circus. It is unlike almost every other building in the world, and people seeing it for the first time show surprise and ask what it is. The answer is that it is the Chichester Festival Theatre, the first arena theatre in Britain with a stage thrust out from one wall so that the audience enwraps it on three sides. The idea of building such an improbable theatre in this unlikely place came to me on a cold, blustery January evening in 1959. My wife Carol might easily have given it as her opinion that this was an eccentric or even mad scheme, coming as it did from someone who was unacquainted with the theatrical profession and who until a few moments before had never thought of building a theatre, or known of the uses of thrust stages. Had she done so I should have let the matter drop, and today there would be no Chichester Festival Theatre. Instead she offered cautious encouragement.

How did this futuristic plan leap into the mind of a theatrical innocent? I have to confess that it grew out of the most ordinary domestic scene imaginable. With the south-west wind whistling about the rooftop, I sat by a glowing fire on that evening of January 4, 1959, with Carol and my sons David, then 23, and Barry, 20. Carol was knitting, Barry was playing patience, David was reading. The television set was turned on, tuned to BBC, and I was half-reading, half-viewing as Huw Wheldon appeared on the screen to present his programme *Monitor*, in which he reviewed the latest achievements in the arts. Within a few minutes I laid down my book and gave *Monitor* my absorbed attention.

The programme's subject was the story of a theatre in Canada, the Stratford, Ontario, Shakespeare Theatre, told by an interview with Dr. (now Sir) Tyrone Guthrie, the renowned theatrical producer. A short piece of film showed a battle scene from Guthrie's production of *Henry V* on the Ontario theatre's thrust stage.

As a fairly regular theatre-goer in Brighton, Portsmouth and London, and founder 25 years previously of the Chichester Players, an amateur group, I was naturally interested in the lively possibilities of the new-shaped theatre. But what truly enthralled me was the history, related by the master story-teller Guthrie, of the community effort behind the realisation of the Stratford venture. Here were ordinary people in a remote Canadian town playing a life-sized game of Snakes and Ladders and, after many ups and downs, reaching home.

The full story of the Stratford, Ontario, Shakespeare Theatre is entertainingly told by Tyrone Guthrie and Robertson Davies in three books, *Renown at Stratford*, *Twice have the Trumpets Sounded* and *Thrice the Brinded Cat Hath Mew'd*. Tom Paterson, a journalist, had put the idea to his friends, arguing that as their town had the same name as Shakespeare's birthplace there ought to be a theatre there, as at Stratford-upon-Avon, to perform his works. Stratford, Ontario, was only a small town, of 20,000 inhabitants. The fact that this exactly matched the population of Chichester was one of the first points to capture my attention. Cities of the size of Manchester or Birmingham would obviously have the resources to build a theatre, but for a limited community the achievement would be outstanding.

Paterson approached the local Chamber of Commerce and persuaded them to give him a grant to come to England and explore the possibilities of theatrical support. Among the people he met was Tyrone Guthrie, and eventually Guthrie was invited to Canada to consult with the provisional committee which had been formed in Stratford. To test their sincerity, Guthrie tried to discourage them by recounting the difficulties they would face if they wanted a significant theatre. He told them if they wanted simply to make money they could easily do so by promoting a leg-kicking show, but in that case he would not be interested in helping. They assured him they wanted to do something worthwhile, and were not afraid of the problems.

It was agreed that they would begin in an experimental way by digging an amphitheatre in their lovely park and covering it temporarily with a tent. It would be good common sense to do it in this way, as no-one could forecast whether a theatre would succeed so far away from large cities and with a restricted supporting population. If it failed to attract capacity audiences, then they would not be left with a large and costly white elephant of a building, and the financial loss would not be great. Guthrie then stated the other principles he considered they should adopt. His most important condition was that the theatre should not have an orthodox proscenium stage. It should be constructed with a stage thrust out into the amphitheatre to enable the audience to sit around three sides of it.

This modern use of the old Grecian style theatre had been forced upon Tyrone Guthrie some years earlier when he produced *The Three Estates* for the Edinburgh Festival at the Kirk Assembly Hall. In this hall it was impossible to move the seats which, in serried rows, surround the Moderator's throne on three sides. For many years Guthrie had pondered over the advantage of seating a large audience nearer to the stage than can be achieved with the usual front presentation, and he realised that this particular play would lend itself to a thrust stage. It was a great success, and it ran for three festivals. I thought this surely was the exploitation of the third dimension which the live theatre could stake against the competition of the cinema and television, both of which were still fettered to the flat two-dimensional screen.

Guthrie's other demands were for a large auditorium of 1,450 seats, and the services of the finest designers and star actors and actresses. Once again this seemed the way to entice people out of their houses, where they sit in comfortable chairs watching television. The possibility of seeing world-renowned actors and actresses in person should bring large audiences, and with a large capacity theatre you would have enough money to pay for the stars. There must be enough income from box office receipts if the theatre was not to be dragged down by heavy debts and placed in need of subsidies from civic and state funds. Stratford's provisional committee followed Guthrie's rules to the letter, and their venture was a huge success.

As *Monitor* came to an end, I turned to my family and said, 'If they can do that in Canada, why can't we do it here in Chichester?' My sons were enthusiastic, but Carol, though impressed, seemed a little doubtful. Now one tactic married life has taught me is not to keep going on about a thing ; to do so only asks for opposition. For a week I said nothing more, though my mind was seething with plans. Then I reminded Carol of the idea, diffidently asking if she thought a preliminary investigation would be worth while. At that moment Chichester's theatrical future hung in the balance. Had she said 'No' I should have dropped the notion, for we have always worked together in all our interests.

'It will be a formidable task,' she said, '— but there's no harm in looking into it.' I wrote a letter to Huw Wheldon, asking if he could help to arrange a meeting between me and Guthrie.

Chapter Two

BUT WHY CHICHESTER?

IN HIS VERY friendly reply, Huw Wheldon told me that Tyrone Guthrie was in Israel, but that he would be in Stratford-upon-Avon in March to rehearse productions for the 1959 Shakespeare Festival. This gave me plenty of time to think about the project. At this time I kept my thoughts to myself, or at least in the family. To make a public announcement before I had a watertight economic plan would be foolish in the extreme.

Chichester once had a 'live' theatre; it lasted from 1792 until 1847 and Edmund Kean once played the part of Sir Edward Mortimer there in *The Iron Chest*. The building still stands in South Street having been a brewhouse, a gymnasium, a public library, furniture store and now an antique market. To start a theatre in Chichester would need months of quiet investigation, after first making an analysis of the ingredients of success at Stratford, Ontario.

I was determined that any theatre we might build must be a specialist one, and the thrust stage was obviously the one to use with a capacity of at least 1,400. It must use the finest actors, designers and producers. And the building must be evolved in phases, so that we could prove its worth before too much money was involved.

These three fundamentals later became known as my 'Trinity,' as I was convinced that all three must be kept intact; for without any one of them the others would be useless. Above all, it was the style of the stage and auditorium which most held my interest. I had seen many very excellent productions at Stratford-upon-Avon in which the apron stage was used to great effect, and where lighting and the use of symbolic properties had reduced the the need for the usual elaborate scenery.

Theatres 'in-the-round' had been pioneered for many years by John English, in his mobile arena theatre visiting Wales and the Midlands, and by Stephen Joseph with his Studio Theatre Company at Scarborough and Stoke-on-Trent. Stephen Joseph describes his beliefs, and his successes, in his book *Theatre in the Round* published by Barrie and Rockliff. I saw several excellent plays under the direction of Scott Gilbert at the Pembroke Theatre at Croydon, a hall converted for in-the-round productions but I felt that the use of the fourth side for the audience often stretched imagination too far and was sometimes embarrassing for both actors and audience. The Questors Theatre, under the inspired leadership of Alfred Emmett, was being redesigned as a flexible theatre.

The use of the wide open stage at the Mermaid, and on a more lavish scale at Oberammagau, did much to bring in a larger field of view. But I could see the immense dramatic possibilities of the thrust stage, where the audience were no longer peering into a room at its occupants but were, in effect, in there with them. This meant involvement of the audience, in its best sense.

I wondered if others were as tired as I was of make-believe scenery. Pillars so obviously made of flat hardboard, gardens of plastic flowers, and bedroom doors that stuck and shook the whole fabric of the house. Shafts of light could do so much more to arouse the imagination and heighten the dramatic effect of acting. Of course, the emphasis would have to be on the finest acting. If the greater depth of stage produced finer acting, surely this was a challenge not to be shirked.

One of the great advantages was the fluid use of the stage that could be made by the many exits and entrances from all directions — through the audience as well as from back stage. This would mean continuity of action, particularly by eliminating the pauses needed for changing scenes.

Because actors would often be turning away from sections of the audience, greater emphasis would be laid on clear enunciation. Again this would surely be a good thing to promote now that there was a growing inclination to rely on microphones.

6

It would be foolish to pretend that thrust stages should replace prosceniums. The whole idea must be to construct some of them alongside the present proscenium theatres. I simply felt intensely attracted to the thrust stage as the obvious 'third dimension' asset of living theatre, and I knew it would enhance the production of many plays. But the proscenium, the open stage and the thrust stage should all be available to the theatrical profession so that actors, directors, designers and playwrights should have the opportunities and the challenge of each.

Finally, I thought it necessary to consider the comfort and contentment of the audiences. People want to feel welcomed by the management. This calls for a friendly and helpful box office staff not behind a forbidding grille, but standing at an open counter resembling a hotel's reception desk. Smiling usherettes handing out free programmes removes the embarrassment of searching for money in the aisles. I dreamed, too, of a large foyer where everyone meets, no matter what price they have paid for seats, creating a social atmosphere before the play begins. Add a comfortable seat, an uninterrupted view, bars with speedy service, and we should have a theatre worth visiting.

Why should I want to build a theatre in Chichester, particularly at a time when theatres were being demolished all over the country? For one thing, I have never been convinced by the argument that the theatre is dying, and I am quite sure the majority of the theatrical profession have never had real doubts of the future. It was the invasion of property companies, who wanted the sites in town centres for high value office blocks and shops, which outbid the Arts.

Geographically, Chichester was ideal. It lies sixty miles from London, and is approached by routes through glorious country in Surrey and Sussex. These routes were well known by those who came for the races at the traditional 'Glorious Goodwood' meeting held annually on the Duke of Richmond's estate. Universities had been created in the past few years at Southampton and Brighton (Sussex University), and Chichester was a mere hour's drive from both. The coastal road and the railway traversing the same strip of coast made access to Chichester simple for the people of the surrounding counties. At that time there was no City of

London Festival, and the only one in the south was the Bath Festival, which was mainly musical. Portsmouth was only 15 miles away, and there were many other nearby towns. Whilst Sir Laurence Olivier was later to describe Chichester as a city of 'only 20,000 souls, men, women and children,' I knew there was an immediate surrounding district population of 45,000 and the population of the whole coastal area was doubled in the summer holiday months.

Obviously a large theatre such as I was contemplating could not be sustained throughout the year; but it seemed good economics to run it as a festival during the summer, skim the cream during that time, and close down in the winter to save a good proportion of the overheads. To run at a loss in the winter, and then have to reduce standards throughout the peak time to make up for these debts, would lower the effectiveness of a specialised theatre. The festival must be a special occasion which people look forward to, watching for the opening of the booking period and making their plans accordingly. When the theatre is always there it is easy to say 'I must go there sometime,' and procrastination produces ultimate inertia.

For what reasons, besides the ones I have already given, would this theatre be likely to attract all age groups, especially the younger generation, more than the theatres at Portsmouth and Brighton? To my mind it was obvious that modern youth, now being brought up in the atmosphere of modern school buildings, houses and factories, did not care much for the gold and plush Victorian theatres that the older generation was trying to restore and revive. A few museum pieces could well be appreciated, but for regular theatre-going these efforts seemed to young people to be looking backwards rather than forwards. There were a few exceptions, where managements were making successful attempts to cater for them, but on the whole the example of the King's Theatre at Portsmouth was typical. Here Comdr R. B. Cooper was having a battle to keep the theatre going against odds. Ballet and some musicals would fill the house, but other plays would struggle along, often bolstered by his own money. The theatre was in the general circuit of pre-London shows, many of them excellent, with stars of national repute and offering first class entertain-

8

ment, but the people of Portsmouth did not back it sufficiently.

The Theatre Royal at Brighton, with a capacity of just over 1,000, was also on a pre-London circuit and well patronised, but running on a knife edge. Both these theatres were well run, presenting good plays and catering for the comfort of the audience, except for a small proportion of seats with a poor view of the stage. They were in the midst of large communities, but they were old buildings with minute foyer spaces which prevented a good community gathering before the show or during the intervals. Carol and I always enjoyed going to either of them. Generally, however, too much attention is paid to existing audiences and not enough to the possibility of creating new ones. In contrast the world-renowned Glyndebourne was set way out in a fold of the Sussex Downs and there it had proved possible to attract audiences, from far away, for opera. It had been a 'wildly improbable idea', which had succeeded in enticing people to go a long distance for an entertainment and enjoy it as a special occasion. Perhaps Chichester could work as a theatrical complement to it. The younger generation have always wanted to be in at the beginning of anything rather than carrying on the creations of the adults. A new building, therefore, has a greater chance of attracting them. Young people were certainly being attracted to the Mermaid, in the city of London, and the new Belgrade Theatre in Coventry.

What else made Chichester the right place for this idea? Naturally, I favoured Chichester because I live there. Few could live in such a city for long without loving its unique atmosphere, and I had always wondered how we could preserve its importance in the future developments around us in a way which would blend with its past Roman origins and its Cathedral.

Dr. Thomas Sharp, commissioned by the City Council to advise on the preservation and replanning of Chichester produced a penetrating report in 1948 entitled 'Georgian City', published for the City Corporation by the Southern Publishing Company.

The introduction 'Chichester Today' is too long to quote in full but it is well worth reading by anyone visiting this 'important part of our national heritage'. Here are a few significant passages :—

'While all cathedral-cities have a common character, they all have a marked character of their own. Chichester especially has this. In one sense, indeed in the quintessence, it is the least typical of cathedral-cities. Its Cathedral is related to the surrounding city in a most un-English way.'

'But it is not only the unusually intimate relationship of Cathedral and city that gives Chichester its special importance as distilling the essential spirit of a cathedral-city as it used to be and as it is still nostalgically held to be.'

'The city around the Cathedral has kept its old quality in a way that no other place in England has. Here, within a street pattern that was laid down by the Romans nearly two thousand years ago, are all the essential physical ingredients of a cathedral-city in a surprisingly pure, unadulterated form. Chichester is the least spoiled example now remaining in England of a naturally grown, as distinct from a deliberately planned, renaissance town. It is a living and lively as well as a lovely city, living a natural, busy, common everyday 20th century life in its most uncommon 18th century streets ; supplying the needs of its surrounding countryside ; an energetic and thriving county town as well as a cathedral-city. And that, perhaps, is its most special quality of all ; being special in so many senses, it remains essentially natural and ordinary in the life that it lives and in the services it performs.'

Yes, Chichester was a good place to build a theatre. But where should it be sited ? The modern problem of parking cars meant that it should be just outside the town rather than in the busy centre. I had the perfect location in mind. In fact, I had realised where Chichester's theatre should be built as soon as I saw, on television, that the Stratford, Ontario, Shakespeare Theatre was sited in a park.

Some years earlier, Mr. Walter Stride, Mayor of the city for eight years, and a man famous for his foresight in municipal matters, had persuaded the City Council to buy Oaklands Park, 43 acres of parkland to the north of the city walls, and use it for recreation and sports amenities. He had proposed building a large sports stadium there, but unfortunately interest in sports faded amongst the young, and even the Athletic Club ceased to exist. It was the ideal place for the theatre.

At this time Oaklands Park was little used by the public, except a few tennis players and the local football and rugby clubs. Nearby residents walked their dogs across the park, but otherwise Chichester people ignored it as being too far out, even though it is only a quarter of a mile from the centre of the city. A main road to London borders it on the west side, and on the south is a ring road for the west-to-east coastal route. I imagined the theatre set well up the rising hill in the park, where there is a fine view of the cathedral — thus joining the theatre to the city, but in a beautiful park atmosphere.

Chapter Three

IS IT POSSIBLE?

TYRONE GUTHRIE wrote saying that he would see me in Stratford-upon-Avon on March 12. Carol and I motored up under blue skies, lighthearted and intrigued at the thought that action was taking the place of words. We booked in at the picturesquely-timbered *Falcon* Hotel, beloved by American tourists, where the bedroom floor sloped so that the foot of my bed was higher than my head.

There was a message awaiting us that Dr. Guthrie (I had not known until then that he had such a title) would call for us at six o'clock. He was afraid we would not find our way down some tortuous alley to his lodgings. I thought it was time to know more of the person I was about to meet, so I plunged through the streets of Stratford in a thunderstorm to the town library and looked up his entry in *Who's Who*. I copied out a list of his achievements and memorised the rest. The image I conjured up from this was very different from the man when we met him.

Experience in life has taught me to rely very much on my first impressions, and whenever I had tried hard to distort a first impression of someone I instinctively disliked or mistrusted, I have always regretted it. At the very first meeting, I fell under Guthrie's spell.

His great height, slightly bowed beneath the low black beams of the hotel passage ; his clear eyes benevolently fixed on mine ; the slow smile, as of a kindly uncle somewhat amused at this encounter — these were my first impressions and they have lasted ever since. Months later I realised that our features and characteristics were being quietly but methodically analysed by him and filed for future character parts for his productions. He made these thumbnail mental sketches of everyone he met, though not necessarily to be used.

As we walked down the High Street my six-foot height seemed small against his towering stature. He spent the time solemnly probing into my way of life and assessing it. Apparently he was satisfied with his conclusions, for he cheered up when we entered the alleyway which led to the back entrance of the general grocer's shop over which he had his lodgings.

The front room, beamed and panelled in dark oak, with a floor that rose from the large open fireplace to the window at a gradient of approximately one in fifty, was a perfect setting for our first introduction into theatre life. Half way up the winding narrow stairs, in a small alcove, Guthrie's wife Judith was preparing grapefruits in an odd assortment of containers. We got to know her better at the meal and during her many trips past us as we sat around the fire, when she took the opportunity of adding to, or correcting, many of her husband's statements.

She quickly registered her sympathy with our tenderfoot enthusiasm, but where necessary she modified some of his characteristic debunking generalisations. To add to the unusual atmosphere there was a singing lesson going on in the background most of the time. This stopped abruptly when the door opened and the famous Mrs Gilkes, singing instructor to the Royal Shakespeare Company, swept in demanding to know, in the kindliest possible way and reminiscent of Margaret Rutherford, if we were hiding the cat which had just given birth to kittens somewhere in the house 'she knew not where'.

What did Tyrone Guthrie think of the visitors from Chichester? In the BBC film *Concrete Vision*, made a few years later, he said :—

'So Evershed-Martin rang me up at Stratford, where I was doing a play, and said could he come over and talk. Naturally I was delighted that anyone had looked at me on television — and still more delighted that furthermore I might provoke them into action.

So I said, "Come over. I cannot visit you, but if you come

13

here we will have supper''. He and his wife arrived, and as it was a lovely spring evening in England we huddled over a coal fire and had our salads and a long talk. I may tell you I was delighted, when he came, that he didn't have long hair and three heads, but seemed to be a person with more than normal common sense and a very driving energetic fellow. I felt confident that if anybody could get a crackpot scheme going somewhere, he could, and I was all out to help in any way I could.'

A great many questions were asked and answered on both sides. Where did one get directors, stars, plays and management personnel? What sort of salaries would they command and therefore what were the economics of production costs and box office takings? How long could a season last, and how many plays would be presented in that time?

As I put these questions, Tyrone Guthrie listened intently and gave careful answers. He was obviously trying to show me the difficulties without dampening my enthusiasm, but his great interest was abundantly clear. Several of his questions were fundamental such as, 'Why ever Chichester? No one has ever died or even lived there ; I mean, at least no notable like Shakespeare, so that you could call it a memorial and have pilgrimages to it.' After I spoke of the town's historic background and geographic importance he agreed that Chichester could be a very sympathetic area for a centre for the Arts.

He approved of the idea that it was far better for a theatre to be set in parkland than in a High Street, and that people would value it more because they had to make an effort that would mark their play-going as an occasion. He pointed out the different situation in Canada : there, people had so little chance to see plays that curiosity would make them go long distances, and when they found excitement at the end of the journey they would repeat the visits and become more of a play-going public.

Another penetrating question was 'What are you proposing to do about money?' It was asked in a manner which seemed genuinely to say, 'Oh dear, I hope I haven't checkmated you.' The answer was, of course, that at that stage there was no money.

However, I told him it was my firm belief that money was always available if you worked hard enough to get it, providing the proposition was sound and worthy. I explained that I had already had considerable experience in getting money for charities in which I was interested in our part of Sussex. Especially was this true with the Eventide Home which we had started without a penny in the bank. Many people said we would never do it ; but once the scheme was launched we soon had a house presented to us by the late Mr. George Shippam and his son Bassil. Donations large and small began to flow in, and after ten years the Home had a capital worth of something like £35,000. It had in the meantime given shelter and happiness to many elderly people who lived in it in ideal private hotel conditions.

Tyrone Guthrie was extremely helpful throughout, but it was obvious that he did not want me to think my task would be easy, or even necessarily a success from the theatre point of view. On the other hand, he did not go out to dampen my enthusiasm.

Finally, I asked him outright if he would be our Director if we ever started. He replied that this was a very difficult proposition since it would take us a great many years before we got it going, and who could tell what he would be doing so far in the future. But at least he said he would not be uninterested.

He asked what I would now do about the idea, and I told him I would not be rushing into anything until I had pondered all that he had told me. I should think about it for a few weeks, get a copy of *The Stratford Adventure* film to look at, and read the books he had written of the Canadian theatre's first few years. If Carol and I then agreed that it was worth further investigation, I should approach one or two prominent people in Chichester whose judgement could be relied upon and test their reactions.

As we motored back next day we discussed it all the way and became more and more convinced that the scheme was not impossible. The period of steady contemplation I had imposed on myself for the next few weeks coincided with my decision not to seek re-election for another three-year term of the City Council. I had been eighteen years a City Councillor, including two as Mayor, and I felt I had served the community enough in this sphere. I was certain I could do more useful, and certainly far less frustrating work, for charities in my spare time. Chichester had always had an Independent Council but now that party politics had infiltrated into it the useful work that could be done for the community was reduced by the wrong sense of loyalties. I have never had any use for party politics in local government, and I found my isolation increasing.

On April 16 my withdrawal from the Council was announced in the local papers. On April 18 I decided to test out a first reaction to the theatre idea from Mr Eric Banks, the Town Clerk.

It was another brilliant sunny day, and as I walked into the familiar atmosphere of Greyfriars, the offices of the Corporation, I thought of all the times I had gone through those doors in optimism, or in despair, or in a fighting mood for what I thought was right. Having forsworn it all, here I was only one week afterwards going light-heartedly in to light the fuse of what might in the end turn out a damp squib.

There were several reasons why I chose Eric Banks as the first in Chichester to be told, outside our family. He had always been more than the conventional Town Clerk. He had shown real love for Chichester and fought many hard battles to preserve its unique atmosphere as a Georgian city. Many good features of Chichester which still remain are there only as a result of his tremendous efforts.

A tall, upright, lean figure with white hair surrounding a domed, balding head, his eyes behind rimless trifocal spectacles searched mine in a friendly but slightly apprehensive way, as though he was hoping I was not going to cause a lot of official bother by wanting to retract my resignation from the Council. As soon as he realised that the subject was a pleasant one he relaxed. When I told him of my ideas he at first looked stunned, but it did not take him long to become enthusiastic. He enjoyed play-going and was a lover of Shakespeare, besides wanting a good future for Chichester.

Out came the maps of Oaklands Park. We discussed possible sites that might later be suggested to the Council; I listened to Banks saying 'I cannot commit the Council.' But I knew that he would be ready to use his not inconsiderable persuasion in favour of it. We agreed for the time being to mention the theatre only to the people I was sounding, so that if eventually it did not look feasible, I could retreat with honour.

Encouraged, I called on Dr Cyril Read, Director of Education for West Sussex, who lived opposite me. I knew I should get a sound appreciation from him. He is a broadminded, forward-looking educationalist, intent on keeping our county to the forefront. Sturdily-built, with broad face and forehead framed by plentiful woolly dark hair, he gives the impression of a merry outdoor gamekeeper rather than an administrator, but at his work he has great force and conviction.

Because I had telephoned to ask him for a meeting, his wife, Isabell, behaved more formally than usual. I guessed that she had decided I was coming over to discuss some matter connected with his work. When she tactfully started to leave us alone, I persuaded her to stay and hear my story, as I was intensely keen to get a woman's reaction. I believe that wives are more important than husbands, box-office wise. So many men are dragged to a theatre or concert expecting to be bored, only to find it an exciting experience. Afterwards, many become ardent theatre-goers.

Both Dr Read and his wife responded splendidly to the prospect of such a theatre in the district. Many wives at that time were getting bored with their husbands returning from work and relaxing in front of the television set when the women longed to be taken out of the environment of the house and its work. This did not apply to the Reads, who made regular journeys to theatres in London and Brighton, but Isabell's sparkling eyes told me all I wanted to know about other wives' reactions.

Now to the next test. In 1953 there had been an idealistic attempt to set up an Arts Centre at the Chichester Corn Exchange. Mr George Booth, a philanthropist, had retired to Funtington, near Chichester, and had offered to set up a trust with £25,000 to found a centre for amateurs to have a theatre, ballet practice rooms, meeting hall and committee rooms for all kinds of societies. Unfortunately, it was founded on the principle that all societies should be brought together to form an advisory council, and there is no surer way of killing a good idea than by such elaboration.

As far as I understand, everyone put forward the maximum requirements for the particular needs of their society. When someone else is putting up the money luxuries soon become necessities, as is seen in the present day when theatres are clamouring for increased grants from the civic authorities and the Arts Council.

Many theatres all over the country were inspected by Mr Booth and his architect Mr Harry Sherwood, but the Arts Council said they would not be interested in anything with a larger seating capacity than 350 for a place like Chichester; this was on the assumption that it would cater only for Chichester people and be open all the year round.

At the same time the City Council were considering improvements to the Assembly Room to increase the seating to just over 200.

Mr George Booth naturally felt that the two schemes were moving towards each other and that there was no point in duplicating what the city was providing. He therefore abandoned his scheme, except for a ballet school, and his very generous gesture was lost to Chichester.

Harry Sherwood, consultant architect to the Cathedral, had worked with Mr Booth and was a natural choice for my next sample of opinion. As he had been frustrated by the previous scheme, I knew that I was inviting a rejection of my ideas. But for that very reason, his opinion would be valuable.

He declared himself completely sceptical and was quite certain I should never raise the money. His wife, however, listened eagerly to our discussions, and she appeared more optimistic. But she did warn him that he should reduce the amount of his work rather than increase it.

Despite all this I noticed that he had started to sketch an amphitheatre with a tent over it, in the same manner as the Canadian one. I began to persuade him to have a good look at the idea and to draw up plans for me to discuss with him. His wife, however, insisted that he would not be able to start on it until he had finished the church he had designed for East Wittering. I agreed to wait patiently for a month or so.

Soon afterwards the film of *The Stratford Adventure* arrived, and after seeing it with my family I showed it to the families of the three I had approached. It was a splendid film which traced the

history of the building of the theatre and the first p[...]
Sir Alec Guinness and Irene Worth. It showed Gu[...]
there to meet the first committee, and his discussion[...]
There was also a good deal in the film about their gre[...]
troubles. Just when Tyrone Guthrie and the two stars w[...]
to leave England to rehearse for the first season they [...]
telegrams to postpone their voyage. The tent makers had [...]
to leave the tent on the site unless they were paid. Frantic midnight
visits to people in the district however, brought forth cheques and
cash to cover the cost, so all was well. When they saw this, my
audience became somewhat subdued. On future occasions, while
never minimising the difficulties we were likely to encounter, I
edited the film by eliminating these sequences. I believed that our
scheme could avoid these particular troubles by guaranteeing to
everyone who gave donations that we would not proceed with the
building if we did not first raise a very substantial part of the sum
needed.

It now seemed logical to approach Lord Bessborough, at his
nearby Stansted home. He did not really know anything about me
personally though we had met a few times and he was aware of the
fact that I had been Mayor when the Queen had paid a visit to
Chichester. This would be a crucial test as I was approaching
someone unacquainted with my other charitable work, and this
would bring me face to face with the magnitude of the job of
convincing people outside my immediate community.

Not knowing what I had come about, he was naturally
expecting another supplicant for money. Well known people in
his position are ceaselessly bombarded by every possible charity.
As it happened money was not the purpose of my visit, but advice
and agreement to join in the adventure because his family had
always been keenly interested in drama and had many family ties
with Chichester. Lord Bessborough is a fine scholar and has a deep
knowledge of the classical dramatists besides having acted, both
in England and Canada, and written plays himself. (*Nebuchadnez-
zar, An Adaptation of The Four Men by Hilaire Belloc,* and *Triptych.*)
In 1927 his father had built a delightful miniature theatre adjoining
the house and modelled it on the smallest theatre in the West End
of London, the Duchess. It was the scene of many productions by

19

e Society of Stansted Players which was formed of leading members of the Canterbury Old Stagers and the Windsor Strollers, together with members of the family. On occasion members of my own Chichester Players were invited to join in and there were guest actors such as Margaretta Scott, Ann Casson, with E. Martin Browne and Robert Speaight as producers. Unfortunately the theatre was destroyed by fire during the war by cigarette ends left by members of the local Home Guard. It was a great loss to the family, their friends and the Sussex and Hampshire communities.

It did not surprise me that Lord Bessborough spent the first twenty minutes of my visit telling me of all the financial problems of landowners. I was being diplomatically 'warned off the grass' and I was getting increasingly anxious that I should not have a real opportunity of detailing my ideas, since I knew the family was preparing to leave for London by mid-afternoon. I had packed projector, screen and the Stratford film into my car just in case there was time to show it, but they were never needed. When I told Lord Bessborough what I was contemplating he was extremely dubious that it could succeed. He quoted his own financial experience with Glyndebourne and the Festival of Sussex, in which he presented Robert Speaight in *The Four Men* around the Sussex towns. Lord Bessborough, tall, handsome and possessing a most melodious speaking voice, might give an impression to some that he is something of a dilettante when he discusses a subject in a somewhat hesitant manner. I have found him far from that, and I have great belief in his kind sincerity.

Lord Bessborough was a director of ATV and therefore much involved with show business, was also a spokesman in the House of Lords on Electronics and Space Research and was one of the very first to advocate the setting up of a University of the Air. He became Parliamentary Secretary for Science in 1963; he is more ready than most people to pursue new ideas but he wisely likes to take the opinion of experts before he allows himself to be overtaken by rash enthusiasm. He therefore suggested that he should give me an introduction to Mr Ian Hunter, the impresario, who 'knew more about festivals than any other living person' having helped to create the Edinburgh Festival and the Bath Festival. If Mr Hunter thought it was a feasible proposition, said Lord

Bessborough, he would join in with me. If not, then it would be best to abandon the idea. If we went ahead he would try and get the television companies and others in the City to help financially, which he ultimately did.

On May 7, the day after my last attendance at the City Council as a Councillor I went to see Mr Ian Hunter at his offices in Wigmore Street. Sitting on a hard seat in the outer office near a typist, I waited for about ten minutes, feeling unusually nervous. Was this the moment of truth? Did so much depend on one opinion? Was I thinking in terms of a definite decision? Someone of obvious importance in the music world was eventually shown out and I entered Mr Hunter's office to find him seated behind a large, paper-laden desk, with his back to the large casement windows in the orthodox interviewing position, with full light on your victim and shadow on yourself to hide your own emotions. After a penetrating glance he asked my indulgence whilst he telephoned to Austria regarding what appeared to be a crisis at Covent Garden. A few more telephone interruptions with an international flavour took place during our meeting. I began to feel that Chichester would seem small fry among his world-wide activities.

I prefaced my account by asking him to be quite sure to give a very frank and honest judgement, as I was the last person to go on with a campaign which could lead a great number of people up a garden path. I weighed into the story, and at the end of it he sat quiet, thinking. Then he said that, first of all, he considered Chichester was absolutely the right place for such a festival; and secondly that if I kept solidly to the whole of my trinity of principles I could not fail. Especially was this true in relation to the use of stars. He related how he could fill the Festival Hall any day with a big name but otherwise he could lose money every time. I came away jubilant, as it was obvious that he had spoken candidly and impartially.

Leaving his office I went round to the bombed site where I had parked the car, and where Carol was nearly expiring in the heat of the spring day. As I got in I said that I thought we really would be building this theatre. Ian Hunter, whilst he did not know it, had probably been the turning point in our deliberations whether to go ahead or not. That interview helped to draw together all the threads we had been spinning. I presume he communicated his confidence in the scheme to Lord Bessborough, because I later heard from Lord Bessborough that he would be wholeheartedly with me in the preliminary explorations.

It was now necessary to give the theatre prospect a wider outlook than a Chichester local effort and so, after a letter giving a brief idea of the reason for requesting a talk, the Duke of Norfolk on May 12 listened to the story which was now beginning to become all too familiar and flowing.

Once again it was not money I sought, but support, and recognition of the fact that the proposal could be of interest to the County as a whole if the Lord Lieutenant agreed to be Patron. The Duke and the Duchess, with all members of their family, were sympathetic to all charities and worked enthusiastically for many of them. Enigmatic at a distance, the Duke is friendly and humorous when in relaxed conversations such as this one. He reacted by stating categorically and emphatically that he himself had no use for theatricals. He said he had been persuaded to take part in a great pageant in the grounds of Arundel Castle when he was a boy and as a result of that experience he had resolved not only never to take part in, but never to go to one again. He seldom went to theatres but would probably come once to ours and that would be about all. While he said he could not give any advice about theatres, he could help by his experience with car parking and catering at big events like Ascot, Epsom and his own celebrated cricket matches at the Castle. He hoped we should have adequate car parking on asphalt near the theatre. Nothing could be worse for everyone, especially ladies in long dresses, than having to squelch through mud. You could have a resounding success with your play, but next morning all you would get in the way of publicity would be a picture of 'Lady So-and-So loses her shoes in the mud'.

I was able to tell him that luckily the City Council had adopted a suggestion in Dr. Sharp's report on Chichester to turn Sloe Fair Field, adjoining the possible site for the theatre, into an asphalted peripheral car park for the city. There would be space for 500 cars. (Many people believed later that this was all done for the theatre, and the Council was accused of 'going crazy on the Arts'.)

The Duke's other valuable advice was on the question of catering. At that time I envisaged marquees being used for that purpose, so as to relieve the first phase of building. The Duke's experience with catering for race meetings showed that once you had established a tradition, such as waiter service, people would not convert to buffet help-yourself ideas, even though the menus and costs were the same and the time halved for the meal. It was therefore important to start in the right way.

After a long and very friendly talk, the Duke agreed to be Patron providing he could be released if we did not get anywhere with the idea within three years or so. It is pleasing that to this day he is still our Patron, and this is the only way we can honour him. He has since said that he has enjoyed a few of the plays and the special occasions at the theatre. The Duchess of Norfolk has certainly enjoyed most of the plays and has brought many guests. As I left him that morning, the Duke said goodbye with a look of some sympathy, as everyone else had done.

To complete that day I went to see a heart specialist at Hove, not because I had any definite symptoms but because I had no illusions about the tremendous pressure I would be under for many years to come. I got a completely satisfactory assessment and was told that if I wanted to be a human dynamo I could do so. The specialist said this with the air of someone who wondered why I did not play golf or go sailing in my spare time like other people. In the turbulent years to come, I often wondered the same thing.

Chapter Four

WHAT ARE WE GOING TO DO ABOUT MONEY?

NOW THE HORIZON was becoming less hazy. It was time to explore the availability of money. My first call was to the late Lord Woolton, whose autobiography I had read and who seemed to be the sort of person who would encourage a private enterprise like this. He had raised vast sums for Manchester University and had lived a life of courageous commercial encounters. During retirement at his house at Walberton, near Chichester, he was prominent in the Cathedral charitable endeavours.

Alas, I was disillusioned. Although we had very friendly talks on two occasions at his house and he gave me masses of good advice on how to get money, I was not successful in getting a donation.

His main suggestion was to go out for money in a big way if you are going to go out at all. Ask in thousands and hundreds of pounds rather than in single pounds, shillings and pence. He illustrated this by telling the story of his campaign to get money for the University. He asked a prominent businessman for a donation, but when offered £15,000 he refused it. Asked why he had refused to accept such a large sum, he told the businessman that to accept £15,000 from someone who could afford at least £25,000 would be fatal to his campaign; others would follow the example and cut their donations by the same percentage, and the target would never be reached. He got the £25,000! Perhaps I should have sailed in at that point with a request for several thousands, but I had not yet absorbed the lesson.

In the months to come I did bear in mind his advice, though of course I was wanting much smaller amounts than those quoted in his story. My first real attempt at this policy of asking in a big way was when a friend of mine suggested the name of Mr Alan Draycott, who had been very successful with real estate promotions in Sussex. On June 9 I telephoned and asked him if I could call to talk about a possible theatre in Chichester. I do not think Mr Draycott had the slightest idea who I was, but I guess that one of the reasons he has been so successful in business is that he was always on the alert and ready at least to listen to any proposition that came his way. Anyway, he agreed, and I travelled out to his home at Walberton — which oddly enough was only a stone's throw from Lord Woolton's.

Mr Draycott welcomed me in, shooed the twins out of the large modern furnished lounge, turned off the large, very loud radiogram playing Spanish music, and settled down for the discussion. Having outlined the plan, I told him that I was not at this stage actually after money, but merely seeking promises, as it was not at all certain that I would eventually be able to go on with the idea. Any promise would be on the understanding that if I altered the scheme in any way he would have the perfect right to withdraw. I then boldly asked him to promise £1,000.

He roared with laughter and said he would not mind giving a few hundreds; even then he hoped many other people would join, in which case he would not have to give so much. I sincerely thanked him, rolled up the plans and we chatted our way to the car. Just as we were shaking hands I suddenly looked him straight in the eyes and said 'You wouldn't like to be the very first person to promise me a thousand pounds, would you? If you would thus break the ice for me I could go to others and say Mr Draycott has promised a thousand and they would have an example to follow.'

'All right,' he said 'I will.'

I sang out loud all the way back in my car, and at home my news staggered the assembled family. This was the great break-through, and I shall always remember Alan Draycott with gratitude for this sporting gesture when it was badly needed.

I knew now that the theatre idea could appeal to people as an adventure and that I might be able to persuade them to trust my sincerity and judgement on a matter about which they knew little or nothing.

My next visit was to Major Arthur Clarke-Jervoise at his lovely mansion at Idsworth Park, Rowlands Castle, just over the Hampshire border. Motoring up the long, beautifully-kept drive to the pillared portico, it seemed strange to be coming to sell an idea. Shown by the butler through the quiet, heavily carpeted house, past beautiful china, paintings and antique furniture, I wondered more and more what I was doing there.

In the billiard room I was greeted by Major Clarke-Jervoise, a short rotund man who rose rather stiffly from a heavily cushioned settee. I liked him immediately, and I have prized his friendship ever since. Over very good sherry he listened to my story with great sympathy, for he has always been a patron of the Arts and helped many causes and many struggling artists in Portsmouth and the area around. He told me with pride of his own acting in London (at the Lyric) and in Canterbury with the Old Stagers. He has an extensive knowledge of plays, playwrights and members of the profession, so here I was on good ground. Except for an 'Oh dear' when I asked him to be the next one to promise a thousand pounds, he agreed without a great deal of delay, but suggested it would be better to pay in two amounts if the scheme started. He also begged me not to reveal his name at that time in case everyone else asked why he had not given as much to other charities. He slowly walked me out to the front porchway, telling me the history of many of the racing and army relics on the walls, his first editions in the library, his china in the glass cupboards and his room of Canalettos. He had the gracious way of living and giving.

Next I approached Mr Walter Stirland, a prominent local builder who has helped many causes. A hard-headed business-man, he took his time, and we had a discussion which ranged over the practical difficulties I would encounter. A member of the Rural District Council, and later Chairman, he saw the theatre as a district amenity, and in the end he agreed to promise. Mr. Meigher Lovett also agreed to another thousand after a visit to his house with Mr Jim Battersby (more of him later in the story) who knew him well. These offers, with a promise from Lord Bessborough of £500 (which he later doubled), showed me that substantial money was available : the next move was to form a committee that might become the nucleus of a Trust. I chose those who had already promised money and others who would be influential or hard-working. I have always adopted this principle of inviting individual people to join me. Nothing is more fatal than to ask numbers of societies to a meeting and then request them to form a committee with one delegate from each body. You get the wrong people for the wrong reasons and the whole ship founders on the rocks.

To those already mentioned as having promised money I added the following preliminary committee; the Bishop of Chichester, the Dean of Chichester, the Duke of Richmond and Gordon, Mr Eric Banks, Dr Cyril Read, Mr J. Battersby, Mr L. Hawkins, Mr Ian Wilson (the City Surveyor), Mr Lynton Cox, Mrs Rosemary Beatty and Mr D. Palmer, the City Treasurer.

On June 26, just six months after that January *Monitor* programme, Dr. Tyrone Guthrie came to Chichester for the first time and had a quiet walk by himself along the main streets to sense the atmosphere of the city. Later I took him to Oaklands Park to see the site I was proposing. It all met with his strong approval, and he was particularly enthusiastic about the environment of the Cathedral. In no time he was envisaging, in his own inimitable way, a grand opening of the theatre with a great procession of robed clergy, the Archbishop, two or three Bishops (he is generally accused of the extravagance of having doubled or trebled the number of bishops necessary in his productions) and all the dignitaries of the county proceeding behind banners up North Street, from the Cathedral to the theatre, symbolizing in one solemn act the basic foundation of ritual which, according to Guthrie, is the link between religion and drama.

Guthrie met the committee at its first meeting in the residents' lounge of the *Dolphin and Anchor* Hotel, freely lent on this and many other occasions by the manager Mr J. T. Canderton; Mr Canderton had greeted the theatre idea with great enthusiasm after his experience as a hotelier at Llangollen where the newly-created International Eisteddfod had done so much for the town. Tyrone Guthrie soon convinced the committee of the soundness of my scheme, and coming from such an authority on the theatre, his backing made the committee firmer in its convictions and more

27

determined than before. He stayed the night with us, and this was to prove one of the many occasions when our family enjoyed his wit and incisive outlook on life. He soon discovered that we were very royalist, and drew from us our other beliefs. He enjoyed himself immensely in being outrageous in his comments so as to get us arguing. Fortunately the training I had from my father, which I had continued with my family, in leg-pulling and provocative discussion was proof against these attacks and we enjoyed the encounters. I think the scoring was about equal.

On 1 July I found myself in front of the City Council at a meeting *in camera*, putting before them my ideas of using a small portion of Oaklands Park. The architect's first rough sketches were pinned up on boards, and it felt odd to be talking as an outsider so soon after I had ended 18 years association with them. I wanted only their agreement in principle at this stage, to a 99-years lease of 3½ acres of Oaklands Park at a peppercorn rent; but knowing the Councillors only too well, I was not very hopeful.

It was, therefore, a great surprise when the Town Clerk rang me up almost as soon as I got home to say that in the ensuing debate the Council had agreed unanimously. I have been told since then that if the members had really thought I would succeed, there would have been more discussion, but they thought it would be wise to agree, since once the Trust had built on this ground the Council would have nothing to lose and everything to gain if the theatre were to fail.

Further meetings of the committee took place during July. Mr Ian Hunter joined us in one of these. Once again courage was given to the lay members when they heard the confident opinion of someone renowned in the entertainment world.

On August Bank Holiday I had a memorable drive with Tyrone Guthrie from Stratford-upon-Avon to Chichester. I enjoyed every minute of it, being ceaselessly entertained by his penetrating survey of the districts through which we passed and his character sketches and imitations of the people we saw. Passing through Farnham, Surrey, I stopped to asked a policeman the way. When he had finished telling us, Tyrone Guthrie asked him if he came from a certain district in Glasgow. The policeman was amazed that anyone should so accurately locate his birthplace.

This was an important weekend. Guthrie was to examine the plans which the architect, Harry Sherwood, had produced for the theatre. He pored over them carefully and approved much of the construction, but then he asked a vital question. 'How are the actors going to get from backstage to the auditorium entrances so that they can approach the thrust stage from all parts of the amphitheatre?' This was an essential and dramatic advantage of the thrust style of stage and auditorium.

Harry Sherwood was immediately crestfallen, declaring that as his auditorium would be dug out of the ground there would have to be tunnels. The site was waterlogged at the bottom of a steep slope of the Park and there would be flooding which would entail engineering to provide pumping facilities and special reinforcement of the structural foundations.

I could sense his depression as he left, and so I was not surprised when a few days later he withdrew and suggested that I should get another architect if I wished to go on. He emphasised, quite rightly, that I had persuaded him into preparing plans despite his protestations from the beginning and that he had wanted to reduce his amount of work in a small office rather than set up a large organisation to deal with something of this magnitude. It has always been a strict rule of mine never to persuade people to do things for me, and I do not know why I broke it in this instance. I like giving people the opportunity of helping but immediately they offer excuses of being too busy I have always thanked them and hurriedly withdrawn my suggestion. Fatigue of the spirit is as fatal in an organisation as metal fatigue is in machinery. Many months had been lost, but it was my own fault, and I have never persuaded anyone again.

Now to find another architect. Setbacks are stimulating challenges and I was somewhat relieved that I could now search for someone eager to design the style of modern building I had envisaged. A year or so earlier I had met Philip Powell, the son of a Canon of our Cathedral, when he had contemplated renting offices in a property of mine. I had noted with interest that he and his partner, Hidalgo Moya, had devised the prize-winning symbol for the 1951 Festival of Britain. I had admired their ingenuity and concept of space incorporated in the Skylon, a cigar-shaped metal object suspended by wires so that it appeared to float vertically without any support. When the Skylon was floodlit at night the illusion was intensified.

Thinking that Philip Powell would have the right outlook for what I wanted, I called on his father, telling him why I desired to meet his son again. He gave me his address. Canon Powell was one of those rare clergymen whom you feel you would confide in completely if you had any real trouble, and from whom you would receive deep interest, concern and sincere Christian advice. His son later recalled that his father warned him on the telephone that it would be useless trying to put me off from an interview, as I was a very determined person.

Going into Philip Powell's rather cramped offices on August 13, I took an instant liking to this self-effacing, bright-eyed gnome of a person. He patiently and rather whimsically listened to my tale and to my suggestion that he might like to be our architect. His description of the meeting is recorded in the film *Concrete Vision*:—

'Leslie Evershed-Martin is a big serious-looking man, and for a big serious-looking man the proposals that came from him sounded a bit quaint. He wanted a theatre, a new theatre, about 1,500 seats. He wanted to build it for practically no money at all, and at a time when people were closing down theatres it didn't sound very promising. We found ourselves in the position of being rather stodgy, sophisticated architects, pointing out all the horrible difficulties; but the more he talked about it, the more he looked like an excited schoolboy — and the more difficult we thought the whole thing was. We listened politely, and admittedly with growing excitement. We didn't know anything about theatres, we were bunged up with work and most of our work was with hospitals, and the only theatres we knew anything about were operating theatres.'

Powell showed me some of the work his firm was doing at that time for several hospitals, including a new one at Swindon. To illustrate how they had been refusing work, he told me that they were the only firm out of twelve chosen to submit designs for the new Churchill College who had declined. As partners they had decided to keep to the drawing boards of their choice, rather than become heads of a large organisation away from the field work. He was genuinely sorry they could not take on any more work, but he wished me luck. I was utterly disappointed.

It may seem odd that my turning points are always at the last moment as the door was reached but it did happen like that each time. Just as I was leaving Powell said 'I must say it is the most exciting thing we have ever turned down.' Hearing a faint wish here, I suggested that at least he might like to talk it over with his partner during the weekend and let me know. But I was not going to persuade them. He promised to do this.

On the Monday evening he rang up and said they had decided to do it.

It was far too exciting, he said, to lose the chance of building their first theatre. There was, however, one condition; if we did not proceed with the scheme, they would not charge any fees; but if the scheme went ahead, then they would charge the normal full fees. I said that was fine as we had no money at present !

The only brief I gave was that it must be a building to hold at least 1,400 ; it must be an amphitheatre with a thrust type of stage with the audience on three sides, and it must be as cheap as possible, because I should have to obtain all the money from the public. Except to show them the site I told him I would not ring again or ask about progress. The architects could then work at ease with their own inspirations and let me know when they were ready with the plans.

Philip Powell also records in the film :—

'We had little intention of taking it on. We weren't playing at being hard to get, we were really bunged up, but it was a fascinating problem anyway. We were lured into seeing the site, which was a magnificent one. We were then clots enough, as we thought at the time, to say yes, we would have a bash at it. So Moya, my partner, and myself and Christopher Stevens in the office, started work, inspired at the time by rather exciting meetings with Tyrone Guthrie, then up in Edinburgh, and then there was really no turning back.'

During the next three months while I patiently kept my promise not to contact Philip Powell in any way, I spent the time seeking more promises of money and conducting meetings of the committee to discuss the best way to launch an appeal. It was a holiday time so that it was not easy to get a full gathering. We still had no tangible knowledge of the cost of the building and we did not know what would have to be our target. I now found myself, for the first time, in conflict with some of my supporters — particularly with Mr George Booth, who had experience of large national appeals and City finance circles, as he had once been a Governor of the Bank of England. He led a group who advocated that we should go out in a big way by publishing an expensive brochure giving all the details and facts, with full costings of the building, its maintenance and the costs of production; listing all the liabilities. We should then approach the big banks and insurance companies and obtain their backing. If they supported us then it would be that much easier to persuade others to follow. If they did not support the idea, then it would be best to abandon it. Mr Booth offered me £500 to cover the costs of such a brochure. He had great faith in the advice of Harry Sherwood, whose preliminary estimate for the theatre, with a tent covering, was about £35,000 to £40,000.

My experience had taught me that big organisations were not willing to give money unless they could see some advantage to their shareholders or employees. If the project was going to become a means of providing relaxation and spare time enjoyment, it could be justified in a balance sheet, but since we were unlucky in not being in the centre of large industries I could not believe we should get such support and if we were turned down by the influential City magnates the damage would be impossible to repair.

I was determined to make the scheme worthwhile so that it would appeal to the *real* patrons of the theatre, namely the future audiences, and I was certain that by sheer hard slogging it could be done. I argued that when people knew that big industries or civic authorities had financed something like this individuals shed all responsibility for its future and left it to 'them'. When an individual had contributed to the cost of the building, then there was pride every time in entering it and promoting its future welfare;

32

this is voluntary co-operative ownership, if one can use the phrase without its political associations. These genuine differences of outlook caused a division in the committee, and I nearly had a walk-out. But the situation was saved by Cyril Read who advocated a policy of 'wait and see' until we had the proposals and costings from the new architects.

During these three months I tried out my first talk about a possible theatre at a meeting of the Chichester Players, which was the dramatic club I had started in 1934 with the help of a local journalist. It was a private meeting, for I still did not want any publicity until I had finally decided to commit myself. It was amusing, and enlightening, to watch the reaction on the faces of the audience during the first impact of the news, especially as they were people very interested in drama. They were so obviously longing to believe such a thing could be possible; yet there was a hearty distrust of my idealism. I was plied with questions, but I could reply only with a host of 'ifs' and 'buts'. The vote of thanks was almost benevolent in its sympathy. Coffee afterwards was taken in an atmosphere that was friendly but sceptical.

Chapter Five

CLIMBING THE FIRST LONG LADDER

AT LAST CAME THE telephone call from Philip Powell telling me he was ready with the plans. On November 12, 1959, I walked once again into his office and met a roomful of people all staring at me. They were clearly wondering what sort of person it was who could have thought out this bizarre idea which had given them three months' hard work. Whatever I looked like to them, I was certainly shaken at their appearances, and I wondered whether or not I had made one big mistake in approaching that firm. There was one man in a pale blue artist's smock complete with cravat, another one looked as if he had just come in from the garden after a heavy bit of digging. One lounged up against the wall fingering a handlebar moustache in true RAF fashion; another scowled as if he was angry at the whole business, although I learnt afterwards this was his normal expression. There were others less exotic but they all turned out to be members of a brilliant team of architects, draughtsmen, engineers, electrical engineers and quantity surveyors who had all thrown in their lot with Powell and Moya to work on the theatre plans in the same sporting spirit of win or lose.

The plans were rolled up on the table, and Powell asked me whether I wanted first to know the cost or see the plans. I replied that I had better hear the price first, because if it was too high there was no point in seeing the plans and we had better all disperse. I had been given every sort of guess from £30,000 to £200,000, and I had privately made up my mind that I might have an outside chance of getting up to £100,000 — though I shivered at the prospect of even trying for that amount. I considered that I should not be able to collect any larger sum.

My heart was in my mouth as I waited for his reply. Was all the excitement and preparation and thought going to be for nothing? Powell told me they had seen Tyrone Guthrie and researched the thrust stage idea, with the result that the theatre they proposed would cost about £70,000. This, they impressed on me, was not an architect's pipe dream but one which could be completely relied upon to include all fees, furnishing, etc. provided of course that it was built in the near future as costs were rising every year, the price might rise to £100,000 in a few years' time. It is interesting to record the fact that, despite all the cynical calculations of other people, the theatre did only cost £110,000 when it was completed in 1962 — so their calculations were dead right, for the extra £10,000 was due to offices and restaurant and last minute additions to fire requirements.

Wondering nevertheless how we should raise such an amount, I asked to see the plans. The whole company sighed with relief and the tension was broken.

Philip Powell says of the making of his plans :—

'I suppose it was a bit difficult trying to design an unconventional theatre, and being asked to build it at about a ten times lower price than is normally expected in a theatre of about fourteen or fifteen hundred seats. That had awful worries, but it also had certain compensations and excitements about it. Very many buildings nowadays are swamped with so-called ancillaries. You think you are building a theatre, and you find you need enormous acres of office space and things that are not at first apparently connected with the theatre, and it is surrounded with these buildings and the theatre itself is almost hidden. Here there was very little nonsense about that, it couldn't be afforded. If you couldn't afford to put the dressing rooms in, you put them in a tent. If you couldn't afford a roof, you put on a tented roof, which they had initially at Stratford, Ontario; and it was in that spirit the thing was approached — not in the rather pious spirit of approaching the design of many new buildings.'

The difficulties of underground corridors for the actors had been overcome simply by standing the whole amphitheatre on stilts with all the dressing rooms and corridors on the ground level beneath it. They had designed the building in a hexagonal because this considerably reduced the cost by comparison with rounded sections. All the units of tiers for the seats could be cast nearby on the site and then slotted into the skeleton building — again reducing costs. There would be a large foyer with stairways leading up to all parts of the auditorium. Backstage area would be small because it had been agreed that on this type of stage elaborate scenery sets would be eliminated by the intensified use of modern lighting and superb acting. Dressing rooms would be few, and if extra space was needed for costumes and actors, then for the first few years tents would be erected outside, until a further building phase could be begun. The inconvenience to members of the theatrical profession would be their contribution to the adventure of getting a new theatre to work in.

The plans provided for the essentials of a large foyer and a large auditorium which would not need further alteration; if the public approved of the theatre and the productions then it would be possible to add the other improvements at a later date. As far as the architects knew, the roof was to be the first completely suspended roof in the world. It would be slung on three sets each of four cables, stretching across to the points of the hexagon. The weight of the roof would bear down on the cables, keeping them taut and pulling in the skin of the shell of the building.

How I thanked my lucky stars that I had not gone to one of the orthodox theatre architects or to consultants who would have had preconceived ideas on theatre design. Later there were criticisms by some of these that the theatre was not complete, and that instead of a lay member of the audience, such as myself, laying down the essentials to be achieved, the design should have been under the direction of theatre people and vetted by some association of theatre designers.

They forgot that this area of England already had orthodox theatres such as the King's at Portsmouth and the Royal at Brighton. Just another theatre was not needed and would have failed dismally. Our theatre had to be a specialised one, and Tyrone Guthrie very rightly drummed into me that I should not be persuaded from my original ideas, since he contended that an all-purpose theatre soon became a non-purpose one. The 'in-the-round' director would say it would have been better for his purpose if it wasn't for the provisions made for a proscenium or for use of the building as a cinema or concert hall. It was even suggested to me that since a swimming pool was badly needed in Chichester, this should be incorporated in the centre of, or underneath, the auditorium!

These critics forgot that I had consulted Tyrone Guthrie at the outset and had abided by his very great theatrical knowledge. There was no permanent amphitheatre stage in Europe at that time, although there were several in Canada and America, all significantly successful as compared with most proscenium theatres. It seemed important that we should not be left behind in providing actors, playwrights and designers opportunities to experiment and meet the challenges of this medium.

I found the plans very exciting as we pored over them and each of the team explained his contribution. They had kept to their brief, meagre though it was, and produced a superb example of modern architecture that would stand the test of time.

As I am not one of those people who can completely visualise a building by plans, they agreed to have an artist's impression painted and a paper model of the exterior made in time for the next committee meeting.

On December 5 the large committee met to hear about the plans of the building and to agree, if possible, that we should go along on those lines. I now began to feel the change in the tide of events. In order to get the scheme working I had to get the co-operation of others, wait upon their thoughts, hear their discussions. It was no longer a self directed operation. I must accept that others could help in the decisions. It was to be a memorable time, for I was to face real opposition.

After Philip Powell explained the design and construction in his usual apologetic but competent manner, Mr Booth attacked the plan as too ambitious and expensive for Chichester and one especially likely to fail because of the way in which I was proposing to get the money. This was a continuation of his previous contention, and it was backed by his friend the architect who had been with him when they explored the idea of their arts centre. They and some others said I was mad to go ahead like this; and declaring they could take no part in it, they walked out of the room. Just as Mr Booth got to the door I said that I supposed this meant that he would no longer give us the £500 he had offered for the starting expenses of a brochure etc. He turned round and magnanimously said that whilst he did not want his name connected with the plan in any way, as he felt I was heading for disaster, he would send me his cheque. We could use it as a bet that I would not succeed. I was very grateful for this generous act. Next day he called on Carol and begged her to persuade me not to continue with the scheme as he was sure I would suffer through it. He was genuinely anxious on my behalf.

Luckily when the opposition left Cyril Read broke the deathly silence by saying 'I believe Leslie is right.' He was sure we should all go ahead. Thus the crisis was overcome, and we eagerly got down to the time-table for launching the scheme. Looking back on this crucial moment I do not think I should have given up, even if all had left me. If the design had been mediocre or orthodox, I might well have believed it was hardly worth a long fight to convince people; but these superb plans would obviously excite people's imaginations. Still, I have always been grateful to Dr Read for his rallying call, since most of those present were people I liked and wanted with me.

One day I went across to see Sir Alec Guinness at his house at Petersfield. I found him friendly and interested. I particularly wanted his opinion on the model because he had opened the first season at Stratford, Ontario, with Irene Worth. He discussed it fully with me, and the only major criticism he made was that the stage was a pentagon with the point looking towards the centre of the audience. This he said, would make it awkward to face either to right or left of centre. It would be better if it were rounded or flat across. Later I found this opinion confirmed by other actors, and adjustments were made to make the stage flexible on the playing surface. Sir Alec said that one day he would like to act on such a stage, as there was a great deal more yet to be learned about such production methods. He also agreed to be one of the Trustees.

Mr Neville Blond, philanthropist and Chairman of the

Royal Court Theatre, was a friend of Lord Bessborough, and the two of us went to see him one day in his offices. He gave me a good deal of excellent advice resulting from his experience of theatres. He also promised £1,000. His main theme was that we should make sure we got the most profitable concessions for bars, ices, etc., as these often made the difference between profit and loss on the whole theatre. It is a sad thought, but so often true where seating capacity is limited.

I also had valuable discussions with Mr J. Hodgkinson, the highly respected Head of Drama of the Arts Council, with Sir Gerald Barry and with Mr Moran Caplet, Managing Director of Glyndebourne. Although in the early days Glyndebourne had contemplated doing drama as well as opera, and had made provision for it, they had in fact not done so, but their example of creating a successful place of entertainment in the most unlikely place outside a metropolis was frequently quoted by me to those who asked 'why Chichester?' Although we should be working on a different plane, I hoped our theatre could be complementary to theirs at the other end of the county, and I was delighted to have their interest from the beginning.

The tide was beginning to run faster. It was now necessary to plan how we should approach Chichester City Council for the actual lease of the ground. So far they had only agreed in principle. Decisions regarding the siting of the theatre had to be made. There were consultations between Tyrone Guthrie, Philip Powell and myself, during which I reluctantly had to give way on one of my convictions regarding the siting of the building. I had always imagined that the building should be nearer the crest of the hill beside a group of trees and about 100 yards north of its present position. This would have given the audience a splendid view of the Cathedral, and thus linked the theatre with the city. However, everyone else seemed to think it would be too far away from the car park, especially for late-comers who would either come puffing up the hill or would be dropped at the foyer entrance. The driver would either try to leave the car there or be even later entering the auditorium, to the annoyance of everyone else. People, it is said, would not walk so far especially in wet or windy weather, and the advice was to build as near as possible to the civic car park in Sloe

39

Fair Field. So common sense prevailed — but I am sure the view would have added extra charm to the unusual atmosphere of the theatre in a park.

The Town Clerk, Eric Banks, worked out with me the best method of putting the resolution on the agenda of the City Council meeting in February, and the architects promised that a scale model of the theatre would be ready by then for the announcing of the scheme to the public and the start of the appeal. David Goodman, a local artist of repute, had been acting as secretary to the committee, and I now consulted him about the brochure we should bring out for the fund raising. On several occasions he had helped Lord Bessborough with publicity for his plays and for the Festival of Sussex. I liked his work, which had originality combined with a high literary standard. The Committee had debated the name of the theatre, suggestions being the Chichester Theatre, the Chichester Festival Theatre for the South of England, the Wessex Theatre, Everyman's Theatre Chichester, Everyman's Festival Theatre Chichester and Southern England's Drama Theatre. In the end it was argued that whatever you called it the word 'Chichester' would have to be incorporated in the title otherwise you would still have to add it in to tell people where it was. We chose the title, 'Chichester Festival Theatre', which said everything in three words.

That first brochure set the standard for the literature we have used ever since, and David Goodman has designed and produced most of it. He was also invaluable in the early days with his advice and encouragement and has remained one of the most loyal of my friends.

The year 1959 had passed. It was twelve months since we had watched that television item. Hardly a day went by during that time without the family discussing the latest moves, and I had plenty of critical but constructive advice from each of them. Since it would vitally affect all our lives it was wise for us all to know everything, and much more enjoyable, even though gloom would spread through the house when there were inevitable setbacks.

Chapter Six

CHALLENGE

JANUARY 1960 was a hectic month of preparation. We had timed a Press Conference for February 2 to coincide with the meeting at which the City Council would consider granting a lease. I was introduced to Mr Surkless, the public relations officer for Holland and Hannen and Cubitts, and I asked if his firm could help us with the organisation of the Conference. It was immediately agreed that he should devote his energies to help us, and the whole of their P.R. organisation worked on it as a voluntary contribution to our project. They had no hope of building the theatre, for they knew we should have to seek facilities and they were not prepared to work on that basis. Their help was, therefore, all the more generous.

In the afternoon of February 2 the scene was set at the *Waldorf* Hotel, London, to tell the news that we were going to build a theatre in Chichester. Was anyone going to care? Would any newspapers even trouble to mention it? Would the public outside Chichester think of backing it? Would the Royal baby about to be born arrive that night and steal all the headlines and available newspaper space? I found it impossible to guess at that time whether the scheme would arouse public interest or not, and certainly no one could tell me. It was significant and exciting that everyone who had been brought into the scheme had worked hard and enthusiastically. So far no one had been paid for his help except for the travelling and clerical expenses, etc. which I had paid. Harry Sherwood had not charged any fees ; David Goodman had given his time and skill without payment and the Chichester Press, one of the best printers in the South of England, had given us the many thousands of brochures free of cost as their contribution. Most of the meetings had taken place in my home or in my consulting rooms. The others had been held at the *Dolphin and Anchor* without charge.

It was in this atmosphere of intense goodwill that Mr Surkless and his team had organised the Conference exceedingly well and we were told afterwards by some of the most noted journalists of national papers that it was the best they had attended for a long time.

It was held at 5.15, with drinks. The newspapermen knew we were timing it for the 6 o'clock City Council meeting in Chichester. Speeches were kept short and the object of the Conference was stated at the very beginning so that the reporters could relax and listen to the explanation without a frustrating build-up. There were plenty of 'blown up' photos of the model, besides the model itself, and a portfolio of details for each correspondent.

On the top table were Lord Bessborough, Lord Addison, Lord Brentford, Mr Ian Hunter, Dr Cyril Read, Mr J. Battersby, Mr A. Draycott, Mr D. Goodman, Mr Philip Powell and Mr H. Moya. Unfortunately Tyrone Guthrie had been severely ill so he was unable to be with us. He sent his good wishes. From the chair I described the whole idea, my reasons for thinking it was worthwhile and the solid foundation of reasoning on which we were building.

'We believe that the fascination of TV which is such a great competition to the theatres at the moment will fade off. People will realise once again that live people acting for you at that particular moment, in that particular way, for that particular audience, is an honour for the audience and an honour to the players. It is also very good entertainment, and we are not proposing to put up a high-falutin' sort of educational establishment. We are proposing to give what we, as an audience, want to have, and that is exciting, exhilarating entertainment.

For what it is worth, I am not tonight going to start being thrown to the lions like those people who have been talking about arena stages during the past few months. It thrills us that having thought about this a year ago, and having worked for a whole year, the controversy is raging at this moment on the very type of stage we are hoping to put forward.

To get the money we are going to ask trusts and the Arts Council, but mainly we shall ask the ordinary theatre-going public to subscribe. We hope some people will come along with very big amounts, it will help the way along, but at the same time it is the ordinary person in Sussex, in Hampshire and London and the surrounding counties who we hope will say this is worth doing for the sake of the South of England. This is no starry-eyed crowd. This is a group of men who have looked at this very hardheadedly. We have consulted all the experts we can. The theatre has been costed as well as can be, and it would appear that if we got something like 60% or 65% bookings for $2\frac{1}{2}$ months of a festival of the very best productions, we would meet our running costs.'

Lord Bessborough said that he thought it could even be enlarged later on to a Festival of the South. He mentioned that Sir Alec Guinness, Sir Laurence Olivier and Dame Peggy Ashcroft had all expressed interest in acting at the theatre if it materialised. He also announced that Mr Neville Blond, Chairman of the Royal Court Theatre, had that day confirmed his promise of £1,000, making the fund £8,000 at that moment.

I thought I had made a mistake in arranging for Mr Ian Hunter to follow on when he began by saying in front of representatives of all the national and international papers what a crazy idea it was. Just as I thought we were beginning to convince them. However, he went on to say that 'all the ideas I have been associated with have had this basic crazy quality. Who would have thought a festival like Glyndebourne, in a fold of the Sussex Downs, would succeed? Who really would have thought of turning Edinburgh with all its charm, its east-windy, west-windy atmosphere, into probably the greatest festival of its kind in the world? Who would have thought only two or three years ago of turning a Cumberland country house, near Whitehaven of all places, into the exquisite theatre at Rosehill which Mr Sekers, the silk manufacturer, runs. This idea has something of the same exciting, creative sort of quality ; so when I was approached I gave it all my support. I think it will succeed *because* it is crazy.'

It is heartening when listening to the tape recording of that conference to realise that all the ideals we enumerated at that time were carried out in their entirety.

Quite a number of questions were asked regarding the eight people who had promised £1,000 each, the length of season, travel facilities and the number of productions.

Time was getting on and I began to get rather anxious about the telephone message I was expecting from Chichester to say all was well. Questions had nearly dried up, and one of the correspondents asked if we had any alternative proposals supposing the City Council became awkward. I could only reply to the laughter this caused that I knew the Council pretty well and I was hopeful.

From my knowledge of Council agendas I knew that the first committee minutes to be approved would be the Cemetery and Parks Committee, which would be the one to recommend the approval of the lease. So I had calculated that easily by ten minutes past six the result should be through to us. What I did not know, so go the plans of mice and men, was that there was a special proposal before the Council to present the Freedom of the City to the famous RAF station at Tangmere. This was of necessity debated first.

Further delay was caused by the messenger I had placed in the Council Chamber. Hurrying out of the room immediately the lease had been agreed, he pulled the door shut and the glass door knob came off in his hand. This meant that the Council and public were imprisoned inside and he felt he could not leave them there. Frantically finding bits and pieces, he reset the knob and opened the door to tell the Mace Bearer to attend to the door : only then did he run downstairs to put the call through to the *Waldorf*, where my son David was pacing up and down waiting to receive it. David scribbled the message down and dashed up to the Conference Hall to hand it to me. There was a cheer from our supporters. With a sigh of relief, since Councils are unpredictable and can be awkward for many obscure reasons, I read it out and showed them the first peppercorn to be paid to the Council as rent for the site of the theatre.

Next morning was the first of a great many occasions when we dashed very early for the morning papers to see the results of the previous day's happenings. We had registered. Nearly every one had printed photographs of the model and there were quite detailed accounts of our proposals.

During the months that followed, considerable interest was shown by the BBC and Southern ITV, resulting in my first television appearance. I suffered as so many others have done from nervousness, not, as I had expected, from the realisation of thousands watching, but from the breathless, ruthless timing and urgency of it all and the fear of getting stuck with the same word like 'exciting' or 'project' which is so irritating to the listener. Having a friendly interviewer who seemed genuinely interested in my answers helped, and somehow I generally seemed to project a self-assurance that I did not feel. My greatest fault seemed to be a possibility of sounding too efficient and staccato, so I had to concentrate on a friendly manner. However, there were many amusing experiences to be gained out of it, although for a week or two the sudden urgent demands to appear at Southampton or Bristol or London played havoc with my professional appointments.

On February 15 we held a Town Meeting at the Chichester Assembly Room which was packed out. Every householder received a leaflet of invitation. The Mayor, Councillor W. Pope, took the chair, and I explained the whole idea of the theatre. Philip Powell demonstrated the model and described the proposed building. Mr Scott Gilbert, who was running the Pembroke Theatre in-the-round at Croydon, talked on the theory and practice of amphitheatre, thrust stages and in-the-round productions with illustrations of his own experience in the States. There was real enthusiasm, mainly because the audience was composed of people interested in drama. Anyway, I felt we had presented the proposition to the citizens of Chichester, giving them an opportunity to discuss it — though we did not really have to consult them, for there was no question of going on the rates.

On May 3 Tyrone Guthrie came to stay. We had a full day's programme for him. After discussions together during the morning, we went along to what was to me a disastrous Rotary Club Lunch. I had persuaded the president to alter the programme and ask one of the members to postpone his 'My Work' talk in order to grasp the unique opportunity of hearing an eminent personality like Dr Tyrone Guthrie. This was done with some reluctance, and I should have taken this as a warning that they did not like having to change the speaker. I couldn't convince the president that to give a speaker of Guthrie's merit time to give a talk of some length, he should cut out some of the announcements and resolutions that so often use the precious 'speaker's' time left between five minutes to two and 2.15, when people startd figeting to get back to their businesses. In the end, the president left barely quarter of an hour. It was obvious to me, sitting at the top table and facing the company while Tyrone Guthrie spoke, that most of the Rotarians did not care. Some even had their eyes closed and some whispered behind their hands, remarks obviously critical of the theatre idea.

Tyrone Guthrie reacted accordingly, and was not at his best. He described what the difference could be in proscenium and open stage productions but he couldn't get far in that short time. Disappointed in the reaction he became more formal. If he returned now to speak to them he would get a very different reception, as most of the Rotarians are ardent theatre-goers who support all the productions.

In the afternoon Roy Rich interviewed Guthrie on the site in Oaklands Park, for the ITV Southern Affairs programme.

Roy Rich:
'You are a professional man of the theatre of some 30 years' experience and, putting false modesty aside, a man of international stature in the theatre. Isn't it rather like taking a pickaxe to crack a walnut for you to interest yourself in this Chichester Festival Theatre project? Now why take such an interest in something which is basically a small undertaking?'
Tyrone Guthrie:
'I do not think it is basically a small undertaking. Chichester is a small city but the undertaking is a big one. They are going to put up a building and they are going to do something important in it and this has the possibility of being an institution. That is what interests me. It is not just like getting

up one play, and either it is a success or it is a flop. It is starting something that can have children. It can get somewhere.'

Roy Rich :

'Was your imagination caught by the fact that a bunch of laymen started this?'

Tyrone Guthrie :

'Pretty considerably, yes, but they are exceptional laymen. There are one or two people there of great drive on that committee.'

Roy Rich :

'Do you think this project as it is planned is big enough, is imaginative enough, to attract audiences from a great way away, from London and other big cities?'

Tyrone Guthrie :

'Yes, I think so, because it will be an opportunity to see a good play in a new way. I think we are all tired of looking at theatre which is in a little rectangular frame; we see two-dimensional things from breakfast to supper, cradle to grave. I think we want to get out of that into something three-dimensional, and I think the whole conception of going to the theatre in rather crummy downtown areas with reluctant restaurants and shops shut is no longer acceptable in the provinces. I think people would be much more prepared to transport themselves out into nice surroundings like this. Where you can get a pleasant meal, maybe have sandwiches and have them in the open air or your car, or if you want to spend a bit more, get a meal and make a night of it.'

Roy Rich :

'What about the special design of this theatre, what advantages are there?'

Tyrone Guthrie :

'You are going for complete theatricality, and above all you are going to relate the actor to the audience as closely as possible so that everybody in that house is nice and near him. They can see the expression of his eyes, and if he is signing a document — you know how in plays so often something quite important hinges on signing the will or the death

47

warrant or something like that — you don't have to overact madly in order to let the audience see that in fact you are signing a paper. It is important that they should be close for the seeing, and still more for the hearing.'

Our spirits were restored by the sight of the Park in May sunshine and the obvious interest of the TV team. We returned to my rooms and there met the full committee to discuss all the details up to the present. The confidence of the committee was renewed when they heard his convincing arguments.

In the evening we had a public meeting for Guthrie to address at the Assembly Room. He asked me to leave him alone while the committee members went up to the hall in advance, so that he could quietly compose himself and prepare for what he had to say. As I went I looked back and saw him silhouetted against the windows, sitting at the table we had just left, head in hands, deep in thought — almost as though in prayer. It is one of my vivid memories of him.

The meeting was a tremendous success, with a lively audience overflowing once again into the back lobby. Lord Bessborough had been delayed by a debate in the House of Lords, so I asked Major Clarke-Jervoise to take the chair. This he did in a delightfully flamboyant way which pleased the audience. Having discarded his cloak to the back of the chair and adjusted his inevitable buttonhole flower, he proceeded to shout into the microphone, convinced it would not work, and opened the proceedings by commenting on the packed audience. To illustrate this he then told the story of two strawberries, one saying to the other that if they hadn't been in the same bed together they wouldn't be in this jam now. He then welcomed Tyrone Guthrie who, reacting instantly to the enthusiasm of the audience, proceeded for nearly an hour to give a fine exposition on why we should concentrate on the arena stage for Chichester.

On May 12 I went over to see Mr John Christie at Glyndebourne. It was a gorgeously hot day, and Sussex looked at its loveliest. I showed him the model and explained the reasons why we were promoting this kind of stage, while he fussed over and nursed one of his pug dogs. He was kindly as ever, but I thought not convinced that we would succeed. He told me of his own convictions about not accepting help from the Arts Council, and of his attempts to convert the Royal Opera House experts to his cheaper and easier forms of lighting equipment. He also proudly showed me his own simple inventions for securing scenery, and other items of backstage engineering. We walked round the opera house and went into the auditorium for a short while to watch a rehearsal.

It was shattering to come from the brilliant sunshine into almost complete darkness and hear, instead of the chorus of birds outside the glorious voice of Joan Sutherland rehearsing the mad scene from *I Puritani*. I would have given a great deal to remain there listening, but he had invited me to lunch, and as it was ready we had to go. At that time he was having a sculpture done by Oscar Nemon, who joined the two of us for the meal. Afterwards we went to see the clay model, which was nearing completion. I admired the great skill with which Nemon had portrayed John Christie's face, but could not refrain from a shudder at his conception of the pug dog looking out from the mass of hair at the back. John Christie had insisted on this as a great joke to portray the fact that the little dog ruled his life, but I found it all a little macabre. I understand the idea was abandoned and the splendid head and shoulders in bronze, minus the dog, is now in the gardens. I enjoyed meeting John Christie as I admired so much what he had done and the standard he had created and maintained.

Chapter Seven

CAMPAIGN FOR MONEY

Be magnanimous in the enterprise and go on ;
I will grace the attempt for a worthy exploit.*
Shakespeare, *All's Well that Ends Well*,
Act III Sc vi

DURING 1960 we ran a great campaign to get money. The Committee agreed that building contracts would not be negotiated until a substantial amount had been collected or promised. We had undertaken to return all money, less $7\frac{1}{2}$ per cent for promotion expenses, if we did not proceed, and we certainly kept expenses within that figure. Except for the salaried Development Fund Secretary and one typist, none of us ever claimed expenses for travelling, entertaining, postages, telephones, etc.

I remember the moment when I placed a notice on a door of the room at the top of my building in South Street, Chichester, marked 'Enquiries, Chichester Festival Theatre.' It was an old building with very springy floors, and I persuaded everyone to keep to the sides of the room in case the weight would be too much for the floor. My first secretary was Miss Heather Carr. Ian Hunter recommended someone who would know about the theatre world, and she had been his right hand at the beginning of the Edinburgh Festival ; thus she had a vast knowledge of entertainment which was invaluable to me.

On the Monday morning she arrived I was booked up with appointments and could do no more than show her the rather bare

*This was the quotation we used on all our literature for fund raising.

room. At the end of two hours she came down to me all ready to depart, saying things were not as she had expected. She was used to very busy offices and the hectic atmosphere of festival projects, and this seemed deadly. However, I was able to reassure her that in fact I had a pile of work waiting for her as soon as I could free myself, and I asked her not to judge too quickly. Work soon multiplied, and she was a tremendously loyal and very pleasant colleague in the years to come.

After our fund raising had become successful, many theatre organisations from all over Britain came to study our methods, including people from the Yvonne Arnaud at Guildford and the Leatherhead Thorndike Theatre. We were delighted to show them our ideas, some of which they adopted and sometimes improved by adding ideas of their own. Later on, several other schemes took heart from our progress. Since there was so much interest in our methods, it may still be useful and interesting to others to hear how we raised the money in such a short time when so much pessimism existed about the future of theatres.

At first we were advised to use one of the professional charity promotion firms. We had already been registered as a non-profit-making charity. I therefore investigated many of these firms and individual consultants, but I found they would be of little use. Most of them boasted of lists of tens of thousands of people who they knew were 'givers' and they proposed to use these lists for us at a fee of about £1,000, doing the circularising and little else. We should have to compose the brochure ourselves and pay for printing and all postages and stationery.

From previous experience I knew that circularising was not only useless but dangerous. Once anyone has received a circular and refused, or ignored it, there is little chance of approaching him again without causing annoyance. Either the chance has been lost or he will send a smaller donation than could be got by other means. He takes the easy way out.

One Arts Centre decided to circularise every address considered worthwhile in the local telephone directory. They got scores of volunteers to type, fill and post the letters. After all the hard work and expense they got back only one per cent of the money they had spent. There are exceptions to these instances; but we decided to go ahead in our own way.

Although the personal approach was hard work, it was nearly always rewarding. The person who can best get the money is the one who is not only working voluntarily, but also obviously shows sincere conviction in the project. Paid collectors are always suspect, since the donor feels that part of his donation is going to pay that salary. Collecting cannot be done well by proxy though it is more comfortable for a committee to sit back and criticise results. The difficulty about going to see people is that you start cold on the subject every time and each approach takes a good deal of moral courage. It is easy to find excuses for staying at home that evening and doing something else. I had to force myself every time, but always I came back delighted that I had done it, generally with a donation, and surprised that instead of resentment I had been met with generous hospitality, and most times thanked for having taken the trouble.

My method was to write letters to people who had been recommended to me, asking if I could call to tell them about the theatre. The letter stated that if they did not want me to call I should understand perfectly, but I hoped they would at least hear about the idea before making up their minds. I said I would telephone in a few days to see if they would like me to visit them. That was the moment I detested most, but very few said they were so uninterested in theatres that it would be useless to call. When they did so, I accepted it without the slightest hint of disappointment.

As the scheme grew we appointed Comdr David Bird, R.N. (Retd), as Development Fund Secretary, and for several years he worked hard, co-ordinating the various efforts and sharing some of the lecture dates with me. He also followed the pattern of calling on people that I had begun but being a salaried secretary he found it more difficult at times. Well known socially in the counties of Hampshire and Sussex, he was welcomed in many houses. It became a joke with us that he would so often come back and tell us how, by an extraordinary coincidence, he had found he was related to the people he had visited, or had met them in various parts of the world. In these circumstances, it was more difficult for him to ask that most important of exit lines, 'What will you give us?'

Both of us went out night after night, and at lunch times as well, talking to audiences of every society and association; Rotary, Round Table, Townswomen's Guilds, Women's Institutes, religious groups of all denominations, drama societies. We hauled the two large models in their perspex cases to towns and remote village halls, sometimes we talked to several hundred people and sometimes to only a dozen. If I forgot to mention that this was a spare time interest of mine, people thought I was some impresario promoting a theatre for my own benefit. Most of this was just audience-promoting, but it did produce the odd donation. Nothing pleased us more than when, after the coffee and cakes, someone would come up and say they had made a quick collection as a donation to the fund. These instances and others when one or two old age pensioners called to bring a donation, or school children saved up to buy our postcard representations of a bag of cement for 7s. 6d. were most moving. At the end of talks we found people were fascinated with the adventure. There were always plenty of questions, and the models were surrounded by interested people. We both enjoyed these encounters, even though it meant we were seldom home throughout 1960 and 1961.

From the beginning we tried not to use the word 'appeal'. We worked on the principle that this was all for pleasure and entertainment, and therefore it was only right that people should join in if they really wanted to. There could be no question of support being a duty. We simply suggested that we were on an exciting adventure, and if they would like to be in on it we would be delighted. I always insisted on closing down our work during November and December in order not to interfere with the Christmas appeals of the humanitarian charities.

As we had received several large donations at the beginning, we decided to place the names of these donors on seats in the theatre. Gifts of £1,000 were to go on a 'Royal' row of seats, £500 on a 'Gold' row and £250 on a 'Silver' row. But our great fund-raising winner was the Founder Membership for a gift of £100 or a covenant of £10 per year for seven years which brought us in through tax rebates approximately £110. The names of people who gave in this way were inscribed on a large board in the foyer. We suggested to people that they had, of course, always wanted to be a founder of something or other and probably of a theatre in the making : they would always feel they had been in at the beginning and were responsible for part of the structure. The great bulk of our money was received in this way, and the only problem we had was when to close it down. We did carry it on for a few months after the theatre opened, but then we had to stop, as it would have been unfair on the original subscribers to go on calling people 'founders'.

During the later part of 1959 I invited Mr Jim Battersby to join the Committee. He was the managing director of Wingards, a local motor accessories firm which had grown rapidly since the war. He seemed to me to possess the incisive business mind that we needed, and he helped me a great deal and was a good friend in the early days believing in and supporting what I did.

Not only did he introduce me to Mr Meighar Lovett, one of those who promised one of the original sums of £1,000, but in the early summer of 1960 he got Mr A. T. Smith to come down to Chichester to meet me and hear about the idea. Mr Smith, known to everybody as Teddy, was chairman of Bryanston Finances and he later formed the National Union Bank. His greatest attraction is his cheery, eager approach and friendliness in his social life. Ever generous, he enjoys more than anything else to throw a party, do it splendidly, and watch his friends enjoying themselves.

His beautiful wife, Zsuzsi Roboz, whom he married some months after we first knew him, is an artist of great talent, versatile in all media of painting and drawing, with many exhibitions to her credit in London, Paris and New York. It was necessary at one time to say she was a pupil of Annigoni, but not now that her work is so well known. She is a most charming hostess and a delightful friend to us all.

When Jim Battersby brought Teddy Smith along we walked over to Oaklands Park and examined the site whilst I told him of all my ideas. We had lunch at the *Spread Eagle* Hotel at Midhurst, and over dessert, when he was criticising the strawberries, he suddenly turned round to face me and asked me point blank what I was getting out of it ? I was so staggered at the question that my looks must have answered him as well as my immediate reply,

'Why nothing. I am just doing it because I think it is well worth doing'. He replied, 'Good. I only wanted to know,' and from that moment he was with us completely. It was in fact one of the most momentous connections we had made. His brother once asked me what I had done to him, as he had often seen him in a great many enthusiasms but never anything like this. His zeal was based on the fact that he had once owned the Richmond Theatre, and the fact that ours was an exciting creative venture which he could join in and influence. At one of the cocktail parties I overheard him being asked why he was in the theatre scheme when he rarely did anything unless he made money out of it. His reply was that, for the first time in his life, he was associated with a group of people who were doing something voluntarily without gain because they believed in it. He said it was so refreshingly different from ordinary business life.

He soon got so excited over getting the money that he would be on the telephone every day demanding more brochures and covenant forms, and telling me of the new covenants he had captured. He approached all his business associates, badgering them to give him covenants, although most of them knew little of the theatre, and still less of Chichester. He gave his first donation of £1,000 and lent us £500 for expenses at a time of dire need, a loan which I made sure was repaid later to satisfy his rules of business. He formed the London Committee, which met at his flat. It was composed of one or two titled ladies, debutantes, doctors, solicitors, actors, press correspondents, advertising agents and some wealthy people of all ages. Many of them were not too clear what it was all about, but they were swept along by his infectious enthusiasm, they enjoyed his hospitality, and worked in varying degrees for all the events which his committee sponsored.

It all seemed so strange and unbelievable to walk into a London flat and hear discussions and arguments and to realise they were all about our theatre. Although Teddy Smith was always careful to explain who I was, so many of them were talking amongst themselves that I do not really believe they realised I was the one who had started it, and some seemed quite indignant if Teddy referred something controversial to me and I gave an opinion contrary to theirs. This was especially noticeable when the question

55

came up at one or two of the meetings on the subject of gambling. There was some pressure to take Crockfords gambling club for one gala night for the theatre, but I was dead against this on the principle that I wanted our money to come from people who gave it directly for the cause and could not be hurt by the loss of the money. Our competitions and tombolas were one thing, serious gambling another. Teddy Smith always respected my views on these subjects and dropped them if he could see I felt strongly about them

Another argument which kept recurring with other members of the Trust was the question of applying to the Chichester City Council for a grant from the rates. Having been on the Council I knew that any such application would have provoked angry debates, resulting in a very reluctant possible grant of certainly not more than £2,000. Ratepayers would have thus been forced to pay something, however little, towards a theatre which many had no intention of using. It would have created a few thousand critics who would have had every right to express opinions on the way it was managed. Also, once a local authority has taken a hand in something, people tend to leave the responsibility to them and thereby excuse their own inaction. I am certain that we gained donations of anything up to £20,000 from people who were pleased that we remained a private enterprise and no charge on the rates. A theatre by the people for the people was a well known phrase which we revived.

Not only was the London Committee great fun; it collected many thousands of pounds for the funds. Among the events organised were previews of Antonio and his Spanish Dancers, *Beyond the Fringe* revue, Eartha Kitt at the Talk of the Town, the play *Semi-Detached*, as well as tombola at the Arundel Castle Ball and a night on the liner *Windsor Castle* in Southampton Docks. The committee also brought us many good friends who have remained with us, such as Mr Victor Behrens who later joined the Board; he was one of the most generous and helpful supporters.

Hallmark Investments Ltd, of which Alan Draycott was a director, offered a bungalow they were building near Little-hampton as a prize for a competition. This was a real success and brought in over £2,000. A great many people sold tickets during the winter months and at a stall at the Ideal Home Exhibition. When the sorting of scores of thousands of tickets took place we were relieved to find there was only one winning ticket which coincided exactly with the panel's decision, which had been sealed and placed in a Bank. The winners' moreover, were a young engaged couple who were badly needing a house. This was a very happy result, better than that of our first Fontwell Racecourse competition with a racehorse as a prize. The animal was won by a wealthy racehorse trainer, who got little excitement out of his good fortune. But this was put right the following year when the winner was a man from Portsmouth who did not usually go to the races. Having nothing else to do that day, he suggested to his wife that they might go to the races. He bought a ticket just as the competition was closing, and his estimate was nearest to the number of people attending the meeting. He was the most amazed racehorse owner of all time! Bewildered as to how he would take the horse home to his terraced house in Portsmouth, he readily agreed to have it auctioned then and there, and take the money.

Besides the work of the London Committee, there were many local events organised by schools and amateur dramatic societies. There were cocktail parties, coffee mornings, jumble sales, exhibitions and concerts. Committees were set up in Brighton and Walberton, but one proposed for Portsmouth never got going. As to personal collecting, I calculated that Teddy Smith was responsible for £30,000 apart from the money raised by his London Committee, Alan Draycott raised another £30,000 and I managed the same amount. Those were entrancing days, when the telephone would ring and announce another covenant obtained and I would make another pencilled addition. Lord Bessborough, Mr Philip Whitehead and Mr Victor Behrens were all persuading people to give. Mrs Henny Gestetner joined in with us at this time and gave her initial donation of £1,000 — but this was only the forerunner of many generous gifts and excellent champagne parties for raising money at her house in Bosham, one of which raised £8,000 in one evening in a total of grossed-up covenants. Henny Gestetner has been on the Board from the time the Trust was formed, supporting the theatre on every occasion and being one of those who with kindly, sympathetic eyes would look across the Board table to see my reaction when my ideas were being attacked and would come down on my side; this showed her innate kindness and her belief in my ideals. How fortunate I am in having and keeping some of these friends.

My family had also been hard at work, particularly at the various money raising events; Barry went round getting covenants and David went lecturing, especially at the Students' Drama Festival at Leeds, where he met many of the drama critics and theatre people and tried to convince them about our ability to create such a theatre. His greatest triumph was when he persuaded the Students Union of the City University, of which he was an official, that they should support the Arts that year instead of buying new shirts for the Rugger team. The arguments raged over two full meetings whilst he talked about our theatre, showed them photographs and the model and finally won the day, so that the Union holds one of the founder memberships of the theatre. This from men in a London college, who were mostly engineers, and in no way connected with the Arts or with Chichester.

I began writing to various trusts and industries at this time, and in April we made our first appeal to the Gulbenkian Fund, which was supposed to be ready and willing to help new theatres and courageous enterprises such as ours. Lord Bessborough lunched one of their secretaries for the drama section and myself at his Club and we put our case verbally, as well as submitting full proposals in writing. Although we made several appeals in the years to come, we were one of the very few drama projects in a large or small way that never received anything from the Fund.

We always received refusals 'with regrets' and when I sent a marked copy of the booklet setting out the Fund's aims for helping provincial theatres to bring theatre to the people, bridging the gap between school and adult playgoing etc., which was exactly what we were doing, there was still no response. We have never been able to discover what was the reason that caused our rejection when patronage by the public at large was being wonderfully demonstrated in our scheme.

On the other hand, the Pilgrim Trust immediately gave us £2,500, and the Portsmouth Evening News group gave us £1,000.

Southern Television have backed us every year with £1,000. Brickwoods, the brewers, have consistently been our biggest industrial patrons. They gave and furnished the foyer bar, then built the new bar extension. They have made other gifts too, mainly through the enthusiasm of their managing director, Mr Douglas Barlow. Very few other industries were able to help, as we are not in a large industrial area.

From the begining the Arts Council was extremely helpful in advice and encouragement, especially through the benevolent guidance of Mr J. Hodgkinson, who attended many of our early meetings. I personally benefited from the many heart-to-heart talks I had with him about difficulties with some of the theatre personalities. We used the Council's initial grant of £2,500 each year to pay off the instalments of the Strand Electric installations of equipment. Our Board made a rule from the beginning that stage lighting was a production cost which had to be met out of production revenue; but that is contrary to the usual theatre tradition, where it is counted as a landlord's liability. We therefore could never quite agree with the Arts Council as to whether the Council had made a grant towards building the theatre or not, but it did not matter; they helped us, and did so most willingly on their budget, which at that time was a fraction of its present amount. Apart from these few grants all the rest of the money came from individual people.

One of the most important long term developments during 1960 was the formation of the Theatre Society. Mr Douglas Robertson-Ritchie, a local dental surgeon, approached me early in the year and suggested that a society should be formed similar to the one for the Mermaid Theatre, which he had joined. I entirely agreed, but thought it would have to be formed by a group of people who were not already absorbed in the work of the Trust. He undertook to organise it. There was a quick response and on July 12 the society held their first meeting in the Assembly Room which was very well attended. He was made Chairman. A large committee was formed and from that moment its members worked like Trojans. A corner shop at the City Cross was empty, pending demolition and rebuilding in a way that would be compatible with the adjacent Cathedral and Cross. We were warned that this might happen at any time, so the City Council let us have it free of rent and rates, providing we helped them by manning part of it as an information centre for the city. It is still there after nine years, though it is now all propped up and in danger of collapse. But the Society, besides painting it inside and out, manned it voluntarily for most of those years, answering questions, enrolling members, collecting donations, selling souvenirs and competition tickets. It was a great piece of work.

The Theatre Society organised fêtes, coffee mornings, jumble sales, fashion shows, competitions and has contributed over £10,000 direct to the funds. In addition they started their own fund for a society room at the theatre. Members were given priority booking for the plays and concerts, a big selling point for their membership, which soon rose from 4,000 to the present 8,000. The subscription has always been kept at £1, of which ten shillings goes to the theatre to pay for the working of the box office on priority bookings. The Society was one of the best things thought up and managed by other people, and I shall always be grateful to Robertson-Ritchie for suggesting it, and hope he will always be remembered for having founded it.

Many people, especially those who were retired, found a new zest in life and must now wonder what they did without the Chichester Festival Theatre. I sometimes felt awed at the effect this theatre was having on people. One person came up to me and said 'Leslie you have no idea what this theatre has done to people. I know it has saved the life of at least one person, who is well known to you.'

The Draycotts went enthusiastically into the fund-raising with their Walberton Committee. They held a huge Bonfire Night Party, when Anne Draycott's greenhouse, containing her new-found hobby of orchid growing, nearly got blown up. They organised important horse shows, in the field adjoining their house, and these fully upheld our aim to give people real enjoyment for the money they were giving to the fund. Then they organised a 'Star Night' at the Ham Manor Golf House. There were stalls of every description manned by many stars who lived locally, such as Mandy Miller, David Jacobs, Robert Beatty, Ferdy Mayne and Eric Lander. That show alone raised £1,300 in an hour or two, but it meant very hard work for the Draycotts and their committee.

Other people offered to organise parties and one particularly good theatrical night was held at Mr and Mrs Mason's nurseries at Pulborough. As it was a Sunday, we had to get the champagne given to us so that no licence would be involved. The barns had been cleared and decorated with stalls, bars etc. At a very early hour the barns were jammed tight with people being served hilariously by Vivien Leigh, Roland Culver, Hugh Williams, Eddie Leslie, Ian Carmichael, Kenneth More and Norman Wisdom. Selling was brisk, through the use of the wit or charm of these celebrities and when everything saleable had gone, Kenneth More and Norman Wisdom closed the proceedings by standing on a trestle table auctioneering the nearest thing to hand ... a sprig of dead chrysanthemum. My final impression of that evening was of Norman Wisdom sitting huddled on the stairs of the Masons' house eating chicken salad, looking like the sad waif he so often portrays in his films.

So it was that hundreds of people caught the fever and exhiliration of finding money for us and watching it mount up as the months went by. It is impossible to pay tribute individually, especially to all of the members of the Theatre Society, but everyone can take pride in what was achieved.

Chapter Eight

OPPOSITION

DURING 1960 A situation arose over the need for a swimming pool in Chichester. As far back as 1950, the proposition to build one had been lost in the Council by one vote — that of a local medical practitioner councillor, who thought such baths were a danger to health. I had voted for it as I have a belief in inland swimming pools, being grateful for having learnt to swim in the Croydon baths. When I discussed it with the doctor afterwards, he admitted that he had been mistaken to vote against it, as he had now found out more about the chlorination of public baths. So the issue was lost until now, when the idea was being pressed again by an energetic committee under the the chairmanship of Mr David Thomas. They decided to force the issue by raising half of the cost voluntarily, so that the Council could hardly refuse to find the balance. I sent my donation on the very first day the appeal was launched.

When the committee found it hard going to get the money, some of its supporters began to say that it was the theatre fund-raising which was knocking their effort, and there was the implied suggestion that we were against the pool. Nothing could have been more absurd because in the main the two funds could be supported by entirely different sections of the public. The pool could only have an interest to local supporters, whereas the theatre would interest subscribers in all the counties around.

To the local press, a correspondent asked what was going on behind the scenes regarding the Festival Theatre which it was proposed to erect in Oaklands Park. How much did the Council know of this latest development? It had already handed over a considerable slice of Chichester to the sponsors of the theatre without prior warning to the citizens or ratepayers and judging by the articles which had appeared in the press from time to time the Council's action could be justifiably criticised.

He pointed out that the Sloe Fair Field, previously a very useful source of income by way of letting to circuses and fair proprietors was now in the process of a £25,000 conversion to a non-earning public car park which was near the theatre. There seemed to be plenty of good fortune for the Theatre Trust. It had been allowed to occupy spacious committee rooms at Barrett's bookshop right in the centre of the city. This was Council property, and he wondered how many peppercorns were being paid in rent. He had read in the London Press that the theatre was to have its own swimming pool but the local committee knew nothing of it. After years of frustration the city's own Swimming Pool Appeal was going well. If the theatre was to have a pool it showed that someone in authority had sold them down the river.

Needless to say there had never been any thought of our own swimming pool, the considerable slice of Chichester was a mere 3½ acres, and the circuses still come to the Sloe Fair Field, pleased to be on tarmac instead of the previous mud. The car park is used by hundreds of cars every day because the drivers cannot find anywhere else to park.

David Thomas and I agreed that these insinuations must stop, so we agreed a joint statement published in the press saying that the two schemes were not in competition, or antagonistic in any way, but in fact, each organisation recognised the worthiness of both ideas for the city. The editor of the local paper suggested it was the work of 'professional trouble makers'. David Thomas added that he hoped these people would use their energies to help instead of hindering. It stopped the open attacks.

Interviewers reported their findings in various magazines :-

'I'd have preferred a swimming pool' said a pretty 15 year old waitress, 'I mean a theatre is more for the old people, isn't it, and I think the building is an absolute monstrosity.'

A 20 year old telephonist thought only people from outlying snobby areas like Bosham would bother to go, 'It won't mean a a thing to the working people of Chichester.'

The older people were sceptical or downright disapproving. 'I give it three years' said a hotel porter. 'It's only a novelty, you see, anyway there's nowhere for people to stay, we're turning people away in the summer as it is, with just the Cathedral and the Roman remains.'

An elderly woman in a print dress was angry. 'I think it's an appalling waste of money. There's no place for new theatres in this day and age, they should have put all that money into building a hospital. But you can't say what you think in this town. . . . it isn't safe.'

The young men were more favourable. A 34 year old factory worker said 'I don't like Shakespeare, so I'm glad they're not doing any of that, but I like a straight play so I might go.'

Another 27 year old said he would definitely buy tickets, it all sounded very modern and exciting.

But an older man said 'Chichester's been a quiet place till now . . . I hate the thought of the trippers.'

'Why don't they do things like Brian Rix, he's the one I like and people would go to see him,' said one member of the City Council.

These were of course the minority views. There was great interest and approval from many Cicestrians, but unfortunately they never write to the papers and so public opinion can easily appear to be distorted. It is a phenomenon which is difficult to understand but every town that stages a festival gets the same nonsense. Edinburgh still suffers from it and some people utter the same objections every season because they do not appreciate the indirect benefits they receive in the prosperity and renown of the city. Bath has the same reactions and in Stratford, Ontario, they had organised opposition, so we were luckier than most.

Having been in public life a considerable time one gets accustomed to criticism and misrepresentation. One instance of being admonished for something quite unintended and really nothing to do with me was a letter which noted that *The Tatler* had quoted me as saying the reason for closing the theatre building site to the public was that 'children could not be expected to understand that they may not jump on all the seats or scrape muddy shoes on the carpets'. The writer felt that this played into the hands of the wilfully disobedient and provided them with an excuse when caught. The writer thought that as soon as the child was old enough to reach the theatre, unescorted, his parents should have trained him in his own home. The writer finished by contending that if we went on being weak and setting such low standards children would respond accordingly. We should train children by treating them as civilised beings and expect civilised behaviour in return.

It never annoyed me if anyone said they did not believe the scheme could succeed. I realised how impossible it seemed to some. I was also told that local bank managers had pronounced that we should be bankrupt very quickly.

One keen Rotarian has since told me that he collected three bottles of champagne and twelve bottles of beer when the theatre was actually opened, as the result of bets he had with those who said the theatre scheme would never come off. At one Women's Institute near Chichester I found the audience unusually quiet. They told me afterwards that the lady of the manor had declared herself against the theatre scheme, and they did not like to offend her by seeming interested. That really was an exception, as most Women's Institute gatherings were most enthusiastic. Despite the difficulties the fund raising began to snowball as more people heard about it from informed sources.

Chapter Nine

THE TIME HAS COME?

THE FIRST REAL theatre Trust meeting took place in a committee room of the House of Lords on June 21, 1960, when those present were the Duke of Richmond and Gordon, Lord Bessborough, Lord Addison, Lord Brentford, the Lord Bishop of Chichester, the Dean of Chichester, Mrs Gestetner, Mr Alan Draycott, Mr Ian Hunter, Mr Meigher Lovett, Mr A. T. Smith and Mr W. Stirland with Mr John Widdows as Hon. Solicitor. Lord Bessborough was made Chairman and I was Vice Chairman.

About £15,000 had now been donated, and a debate took place as to when the Trust would be ready to agree to building. Some wanted to see the whole amount in the bank, or promised by covenants, before agreement was made; but in the end it was decided to collect £35,000 before fixing a starting date. Teddy Smith was very anxious for us to go ahead, contending that much more would come in once we began to build. Later he was proved entirely correct, for the rate of donations was much faster during the building than at any other time. He tried hard to get the Trust to agree by himself offering a £10,000 loan to bridge the gap. But while they thanked him, they would not advance the date.

I had not expected that we should be discussing such an early start, and I was fairly shaken that we had come so near the brink, but was relieved that we were not to have the anxiety of starting with so little real money.

The next meeting was also at the House of Lords on July 14, and except for the absence of the Duke of Richmond and Gordon and the Dean, the same people were there with the addition of Major Clarke-Jervoise. £22,000 had now been raised, and Lord

Bessborough reported thet Mr Gerald Glover, who was closely associated with McAlpine, the contractors, had said that the firm might consider building for us for a first payment of £30,000 and the balance over eight years with nominal interest. This was news. No other contractor was inclined to help by agreeing to long payments, and we could hardly have a better contractor or better terms. Our seven year covenants could eventually cover this if we had enough to gross up the full amount.

Things suddenly looked exciting again, and I really wondered if we might get the go-ahead well before I had expected it, especially as Teddy Smith again renewed his offer to make up the £35,000 by a loan. One of the trustees, a millionaire, unfortunately started a description of all the difficulties; he warned of the possibility of failing to get any more donations, illustrating this by a depressing account of a failure he had been connected with in trying to raise money for a nursing home. I pointed out the difference in popularity of a theatre compared with something people now thought was, or should be, covered by the National Health Service. But the damage was done. Trustees began to get frightened regarding their own personal liabilities and reputations, and one eminent trustee hurriedly left for another engagement, placing a note in front of me to say that he could not possibly agree to any resolution to proceed. This was all very understandable, and I had to agree that I felt we were rushing it too quickly. If a decision had been taken we might almost have started building that year and opened in 1961. The contractor was ready and willing to negotiate immediately, the building would have been at the original cost, and very probably Tyrone Guthrie would have been the first director, because this timing would have fitted in well with his waiting for a theatre to be built for him in Minneapolis.

I wrote telling him that the date was still uncertain and that our theatre would obviously not be built that year, so that he might free himself for other things. Later I remembered walking up and down our garden with him one day while he told me of the plans to build the Minneapolis theatre, later to be called the Tyrone Guthrie Theatre. He had been touring America, looking at various University sites for a proposed theatre scheme and had eventually settled on Minneapolis. The money involved would mostly be coming from a millionaire. I asked him, supposing we had been able to offer him exactly the same facilities and the circumstances had been exactly equal, which theatre would he have chosen to direct? He said that Minneapolis would win, as after all Chichester was for him somewhat of a repetition of Stratford, Ontario, though of course it would be grand to have such a theatre in England. He felt that America and Canada were going to be the most powerful countries in the future world, but they needed cultural backgrounds and artistic development to give them balance to rule wisely. If he could add his little contribution to this he felt he had a duty to do so. I knew then that I could not hope for him to be with us in the future.

Pressure to start building now waned as negotiations got under way with McAlpine. Many meetings took place between our architects' group and McAlpine's engineers, while the conditions of payment were thrashed out with Mr Gerald Glover, Lord Brentford and some of the trustees. First of all McAlpine said it could not be done under £95,000. We were depressed to think that our increasing fund was simply going to chase a further goal, but in 24 hours our architects said the estimate was incorrect and that McAlpine had not had the time to cost the job in detail. Then McAlpine declared that they did not think the theatre could be built as designed, especially the roof, and they wanted to re-design it. More hectic consultations took place over many weeks. At last our engineers convinced them that this exciting form of suspension could be practicable. Again we sighed with relief. In the end our team was proved right in costing and construction, and the original plans were never altered from the first day I saw them. The only difference was that our engineers substituted rods for cables in the roof as an economy measure.

An interval of four months elapsed before the third Trust meeting on November 23. I was determined we should not meet again in the House of Lords, where we had had two depressing meetings with all decisions delayed, however rightly. Looking back, it is now obvious that we could not really have built earlier

68

than we did. But the reasons given were based more on lack of faith in the whole project than the practicalities of building. It was deadly dull and dreary in those committee rooms, and there was a sombre air of a place where nothing is done until it is on the brink of being too late.

We arranged to meet in the more modern atmosphere of a Board Room at the Grosvenor Hotel, Victoria. I decided to have detailed discussions individually with each of the trustees before the meeting, so that their knowledge would be complete on all aspects of the situation, as it was obvious this meeting might be decisive. One member refused to see me, and asked to withdraw from the Trust, saying he felt it was quite wrong for me to go round persuading people in advance. He had completely misunderstood my motive, he did not really know me, and had attended only the first meeting when everything looked very shaky. I wrote him an explanation but it was no use, and I think he believed we were on a hopeless task. That morning I also had a full discussion with Teddy Smith, then went on to Ian Hunter to discuss the next moves for staff if the go-ahead was given. After that I went to see Sir Alec Guinness in his dressing room at the Haymarket Theatre where he was playing the part of Lawrence of Arabia in the play *Ross*. This was the first time I had been in a professional dressing room before a show, and it was particularly kind of him to suggest it when most actors cannot bear to have anyone around at such a time. As he made up we discussed the various people I might approach to direct the theatre. He suggested Antony Quayle. After that I met my son David and we went along to the Trust meeting expecting to have a most momentous debate.

We now had £34,000 in cash and grossed-up covenants — close to the amount agreed as being the decisive figure. At the meeting there was considerable discussion by several trustees who by their position, or because of past experiences, rightly felt they must be careful with a project to which they gave their names. I could not complain, since it had been my own idea to have a Trust of worthy people to guarantee that the public money which had been given to us for a specific purpose would be correctly used. At last, however, after the debate had swayed back and forth, Major Clarke-Jervoise strongly advocated going ahead, and thus the day was saved. It was agreed to honour our first resolution that £35,000 should be the starting point and that contracts be entered into with McAlpine to commence building on May 1 next year (1961). There were congratulations all round and David and I went off in a taxi, hardly able to conceal our excitement that after all the thought, worry and work, the scheme was going to come to fruition. I felt a great upsurge of happiness, such as seldom happens in one's life. We had seats to see Alec Guinness in *Ross* that evening. As we walked down Lower Regent Street I could see Carol standing outside the Haymarket Theatre with a slightly worried look, wondering what news we would bring. After all, it was due in great part to her that we ever started on the idea. I dashed up to a flower seller nearby, grabbed a bunch of violets and with a flourish presented them to her. Without asking, she could see that all was well. It was a gay evening as we watched Alec Guinness's superb characterisation of someone who had always been one of my heroes and finished a memorable day with a celebration dinner.

Press and TV over the next few days gave us splendid coverage. Lord Bessborough made an excellent broadcast. Tyrone Guthrie sent a telegram from Ontario wishing us well and expressing his great pleasure that now all doubts had been allayed. The campaign to get money was intensified every day, and it gained impetus : for now there were no more 'ifs' and 'buts', and no more need for promises to return money.

Chapter Ten

MANAGER OR REFEREE?

IT WAS ABOUT THIS time that we decided to divide up the work amongst the members of the Board. Teddy Smith and Philip Whitehead interested themselves in the financial aspects of the Building Fund, controlling and advising on expenditure. Alan Draycott and Jim Battersby watched over the building contracts and day to day progress, David Biart consulted with Lord Brentford and Sam Lyons, a well known London solicitor who was also a trustee on all legal matters, while I, as Chairman and the designer of the original blueprint of the scheme dealt with formation of the establishment for the theatre and general policy. Each section reported at all Board meetings and submitted their plans for general discussion and approval. All members of the Board were also engaged on the continual search for funds. Lord Bessborough, by virtue of his many parliamentary and technical interests, and Mrs Gestetner through her social and commercial associations helped all the sections of our work.

At the end of 1960 I had begun to consider the question of staff for the theatre. The first important appointment would be a Director or General Manager. Having read the three Stratford (Ontario) books and discussed the matter with Tyrone Guthrie, I decided to meet Mr Cecil Clarke, who had been the general manager in Ontario. He seemed to be just the person we needed. He had organised the whole of the detailed side of productions, wardrobe and administration at Stratford, and was now working for H. M. Tennent at ATV, casting the drama section and producing television plays.

Mr Clarke was interested in the prospect of managing

our theatre, and I discussed with him the best way to create a management structure. He eventually produced a memorandum which he brought to a committee meeting. It went into detail on costing of management, productions, maintenance, wardrobe, and personnel. This was the first real set of statistics I had been able to get which would apply to the Chichester Festival Theatre.

He proposed that someone like himself should be in full charge of the theatre productions in an administrative capacity and engage a director or directors to work under him. Here I differed.

My own belief was that a theatrical director should be in full charge, able to use his artistic inspiration and ability within a given budget agreed by the Board, and that this director should engage a general manager and all other subordinate personnel. I found this was the conviction of all other theatre people I consulted, and they further stressed that a really first-class director would not work under an administrator.

It was most unfortunate that at this very meeting with Cecil Clarke in Chichester, he encountered a very disorganised agenda. While he was there, Lord Bessborough rang up to tell me there were good possibilities of McAlpine building the theatre on extended terms if I would go up to London to see them. This was very exciting and unexpected news which naturally provoked an intensive debate on the whole situation, so that I should be fully briefed when I went with Lord Bessborough and one or two others of the committee. There was little time to discuss Cecil Clarke's memorandum and he left feeling that we were not really organised and would be unreliable partners. I deeply regretted this; I guessed his feelings, but it was just one of those unusual situations. Most meetings were run meticulously and I always arranged to deal with everything in correct priority.

A few days later I received a letter saying that Mr Clarke had decided to stay with Tennents. Since he went on to a very successful career in television producing, he was probably right.

By the end of 1960 I was still seeking advice, visiting many theatre personalities to get their opinions. All agreed on the need for a top director. I called on Sybil Thorndike and Sir Lewis Casson in their dressing rooms when they were appearing in *Waiting in the Wings*, and on Peggy Ashcroft at Stratford-upon-Avon after her

72

performance in *The Duchess of Malfi*. I had lunch next day with her, Peter Hall and his wife, Lesley Caron. Whilst Lesley Caron seemed preoccupied with her thoughts of the rehearsals she was engaged in, Peggy Ashcroft was genuinely interested in the Chichester idea and most helpful with advice. Peter Hall, on the other hand, was calculating all the time on what use Chichester might be to him and the profession and whether it would amount to any sort of competition. He offered possibilities of exchanges of stars between us, but most of the time I expect he was thinking this could only be a one-way traffic from them to us, possibly as a short term relief for anyone in the company not involved with a production at Stratford. This was before the Aldwych alternative in London was fully under way.

Hall was keen to see the model in the early evening after rehearsals. I turned up at his office to find him in hectic discussions with London lawyers about one of their stars, who wanted to end his contract with Stratford in order to accept a film invitation. Despite these interruptions, Hall studied the model with extreme care, squatting down at every angle to measure sight lines. He then blandly told me he had been thinking of giving Stratford a thrust stage, with the audience wrapped well round it, more than was possible with the present apron stage. He would further urge the Governors to pull down the facade of the building and take it farther out to increase seating capacity for greater box office takings. The result would be an arena type theatre such as I was proposing; in fact he said he had plans to do this during the next spring and so beat us to it by one year.

As he said this, the thought crossed my mind that there might be an element of bluff in this to put us off, as it seemed rather a sharp change of front between the lunch-time discussion and the attitude of that evening. I was a little worried, however, that we might lose the impact of erecting the first permanent building of this kind if his plans did go ahead. In fact, they never did. Whether or not they were ever subsequently contemplated by his Board, I do not know.

Peter Hall later wrote to me to say that he believed our theatre would be the most exciting theatre to be built in this country this century.

On Alec Guinness's recommendation, I had a long discussion with Antony Quayle to see if he would be interested in an organisation like ours. It transpired that he was far too fond of acting and too happy doing it to want to take on administration as well.

One advantage of being entirely unconnected with the theatrical profession was that all my discussions with directors and actors were completely frank. None felt inhibited in these talks, because they did not have to consider my relationship with their colleagues, and I could never be held responsible for any of their past successes or failures. I knew that in a few year's time this attitude would alter, when Chichester became part of the theatre world. Meantime I enjoyed the frankness. That is the way I always like to work.

Only at the Arts Council did I quite rightly find caution and circumspect appraisals, since their role of neutrality must be kept inviolate. On the other hand, I soon learned that you are never really accepted into theatre life unless you are dependent upon it for your bread and butter. Even a casual handyman in the theatre is received more easily into the brotherhood.

As we were getting into 1961, it seemed about time to get more advice from Tyrone Guthrie, so I wrote asking if we could come over to Ireland to see him. On January 7 Carol and I left by plane for Belfast. I particuarly remember that flight because it was the occasion of one of the most gorgeous sunsets I have ever seen from a plane. Besides the usual rolling cotton wool prairies there were huge tufts of billowing turbulence which resembled atomic bomb effects. All deep red or antique gold. We came down from this fantasy with a bump, as we reached the airport in a hurricane storm of sleet and torrential rain with the plane tilting crazily at all angles. The wheels touched the ground but the aircraft shot up again at a very steep angle.

The pilot apologised and said he would try once more, but if he failed we should have to go on to Shannon. Luckily he made it, so we met Judith Guthrie as arranged at the airport lounge. I think she had been very shaken on seeing the first attempt to land.

We drove down across the border to the Guthrie home at Doohat in County Monaghan and stopped at their nearest town to get a bottle of whiskey so that I should not arrive empty handed. I entered the inn with Judith as escort and had my first glimpse of the very dark and, to me, extremely dreary wooden, high-backed stalls of an Irish country pub; it seemed a place ordained to heavy drinking sessions.

We arrived at Doohat in the dark, so it was not until next morning that we saw the solemn beauty of the woods, the lake and the open lawns of this piece of Ireland. We had a hint of the countryside by the posy of *Mahonia Bealei* with its sweet smell of lilies of the valley, by the side of the bed; by this token, and the blazing coal fire to undress by the previous evening, we knew that we were welcomed most warmly. The friendship and interest shown in us has remained as a very happy memory for us ever since.

Tyrone Guthrie had decided that we should not talk about the theatre until mid-morning the first day, so the evening meal when we arrived, and the breakfast the following morning, were accompanied by conversations probing into each other's backgrounds, and particularly into their ancestry. The Guthries did not seem to have a routine of living, but rather a living by custom as was revealed in the bald statement that all visitors helped with the washing up after meals, and we joined in procession to a great stone flagged kitchen, of mediaeval appearance. There at various stations along the huge scrubbed-wood table, we dutifully did our stint, drying plates handed on from Tyrone Guthrie, rather like a bucket chain at a fire, whilst he gave a running commentary on the history of the house.

We enjoyed this mode of life, which was imposed for economic reasons: unless everyone helped with the work, the running of the place would have been beyond the several elderly retainers whom Tyrone Guthrie felt it his joy and duty to care for.

During Sunday morning Tyrone Guthrie helped me to select a short list of possible directors. I showed him the unofficial list from the Arts Council, and we went through the names, grouping them into 'past and faded' . . . the 'up and comings' . . . 'new but strident' . . . 'good' . . . 'possibles' . . . 'down and outs' . . . and 'impossibles'. As the process of working from the best downwards according to their availability and willingness would take a long time, I made notes of his comments on each so that I could consult it as time wore on. When I looked at my notes later, I decided to destroy them; some comments bordered on the libellous if taken literally.

Many of Guthrie's remarks were tinted by his experiences of co-operation or clash in past encounters. They were always perceptive and mostly astringent, but as he adjusted his views when considering our requirements I knew he was taking great pains to be scrupulously fair to the person and to us. After an hour or two I had a list grouped into first, second and third priorities, or what would now be called 'the top ten'.

He warned me that the search might take many weary months, finding where they were, finding out their commitments and negotiating perhaps one after the other. Then Judith came in with a welcome cup of coffee, and he sat back and shot at me the one name not on the list — Sir Laurence Olivier. He said, 'Leslie, you keep on and on about only having the best of everything at Chichester so why don't you go for the best . . . ask him'. I asked Guthrie what made him think there was a chance of Sir Laurence accepting. He explained that he knew Sir Laurence was tired of the commercial pressures of New York, where he was then playing, that he was looking forward to starting a new married life in Brighton and was probably undecided what to do — although he must be having countless film offers. He thought there might be a chance that Olivier would like to explore the possibilities of our kind of open stage and have a new theatre to direct.

For the rest of the weekend it was difficult to keep my thoughts away from this possibility; but Tyrone Guthrie is not one to debate a question needlessly, and we settled down to enjoy the Monday with them. How could anyone ever forget the experience of hearing him reading aloud from John Betjeman's *Collected Poems* as we sat round the coal fire? Who could do it better? It was one of those occasions which needed consciously photographing on one's mind, and I registered every single detail. Colours, textures, faces, the pictures on the walls, the burning logs, Judith Guthrie with her embroidery, Carol relaxed with her hands in her lap, and above all the resonance of Tyrone Guthrie's voice as he painted the words by the various cadences he used.

It was around the table, after the meal on the last evening, that we teased him into some admission, despite his usual cynicism, that he had been pleased with the knighthood awarded him in the New Year's Honours List. He knew he could always raise the temperature of our feelings when he discussed Royalty. Obviously his lack of diplomacy had cost him dear in the past; he was a great believer in truth challenging and cutting through the trappings of snobbery and caste. Honours have come more quickly to others who were more obsequious.

We persuaded him to bring out the large china bowl filled with the telegrams and letters from all over the world, and we dipped into them as though sharing a communal bowl of rice. As we asked him who they were, and in what connection they had sent their congratulations, he replied in his usual caustic style, with many a good-humoured reproof from his wife. Under all the pretence there was a real pleasure that friends, both sincere and insincere, had troubled to remember him.

Many months later, after he had received the accolade, he gave me his version of the ceremony. Either I wore rose-coloured spectacles when I went to Buckingham Palace on one occasion, or the whole place had received a complete refurnishing and regilding in seven years. He had permission to wear a blue lounge suit, since his great height and physique would have meant a special morning suit being made for those two hours. I wondered how much of the ceremony he noted down for future use in his productions.

The next day, as soon as we had arrived home, I wrote a detailed account of the whole project to Sir Laurence Olivier, complete with the history of how it all started and all the plans of the building. I asked the committee to trust me for a while to carry through the preliminary approach. I then patiently tried to await a reply.

I did not hear for a month, as Sir Laurence had been touring in America. His letter was noncommittal but there were two pages of questions which gave me much hope. Would he, as Director, have full freedom in the selection of the plays, directors, and designers, or in other words, full artistic control? This was an easy one to answer because I had made this an essential condition with my committee, after my investigations of professional opinion.

Whatever lay body might govern the theatre they must not interfere with the judgement of the Director regarding the artistic use of the theatre. The governing board must, of course, be satisfied about the financial control on budgeting of production and overhead costs, which must be agreed beforehand with the Director and he must keep to this. There were times, after we had started, when some members of the Board tried to break me on this; but I am glad to say the principle is still kept.

Sir Laurence also wanted to know if he would have a say in the construction of the actual stage area, even though all matters regarding construction were already settled with McAlpine in agreement with Tyrone Guthrie's ideas. I referred all his architectural queries to Philip Powell, who was able to send affirmative answers and supply many additional backstage details.

On March 4, Olivier wrote saying that he was really interested but before deciding he wanted me to go and see his agent, Mr Cecil Tennant, in whom he had great confidence, who would assess me and the scheme and discuss possible financial arrangements. Whilst this was going on, Lord Bessborough happened to be in New York. He called on Olivier to discuss Chichester, and to give him the background. This was the first personal contact and was important.

On March 9 I went to the palatial offices of M.C.A. in Piccadilly, who then were the largest agency for overseas artistes. Cecil Tennant was seated behind an impressive desk in a large executive room overlooking Piccadilly, and I felt as though I were being interviewed for a job. He and his colleague Ben Travers were extremely charming, listening intently while I gave them details of the scheme. They were obviously judging me to see whether I was a responsible person, belonging to a sound Board, who could work with Sir Laurence.

We discussed the financial and managerial arrangements, and then Tennant put through a private call, from another room, to Sir Laurence, telling him the details and our offer of a £5,000 salary. (Sir Tyrone had suggested this would be a fair offer.) On his return, Cecil Tennant said that Sir Laurence would only accept £3,000, as he wanted to be all in all with us in the adventure. This was the most tremendous news, that he had accepted, and

I was in an exultant mood when I then went to keep an appointment with Cecil Clarke, who had arranged for me to meet Mr Hugh (Binkie) Beaumont of H. M. Tennent at their offices above the Globe Theatre. I had a long talk with Cecil Clarke, during which I revealed that Sir Laurence was coming to us. His jaw dropped, and I had my first intimation of the impact this news would eventually make on the profession.

We went to see Hugh Beaumont, who greeted me with the smiling interest he obviously felt for a theatrical innocent. Halfway through the talk Cecil Clarke suggested I should tell him my news. From then on there was a very thoughtful couple in front of me who were only half hearing what I had to say. Both were obviously deep in thought, and it was not until Hugh Beaumont was disappearing in the elderly lift that, just as his head was about to sink out of sight, he called out to Cecil Clarke : 'I've got it ! He wants to prepare himself for the National Theatre'.

I had the same fun when I told my news to Ian Hunter and Antony Besch at Lord Rupert Neville's buffet luncheon meeting to promote the Sussex Festival. Ian Hunter was also satisfactorily astounded, except that I had the added joy of his genuine pleasure on my behalf when he said "If you've got him, then you're made !'

Arrangements were confirmed by Sir Laurence in a letter on March 13, and I immediately sent him a cable 'The Sussex Downs will shout with joy to welcome you'. We anounced the news to a Press Conference at Teddy Smith's flat in the evening, having told all the local papers in the afternoon. This was the only conference we had held where there was a hitch in the arrangements. The press relations people who were then working for us had given the address as Bryanston Square instead of Bryanston Court, so the press arrived very irritated.

We had splendid coverage the day following the conference, and for some months afterwards clippings came in from all over the world in every language. There was another burst of TV and radio interviews for Lord Bessborough and myself. It was obvious that our theatre was to be of international interest from the very beginning, and I shall never fail to thank Sir Tyrone for putting the idea to me, or Sir Laurence for accepting the offer and for the circumstances of his career at that time which made this the right

79

moment when he wanted to do something new. I fervently hoped that I should find him possible to work with ; otherwise the following years would be very trying. Those who knew him told me we should get on well together, but I must admit to considerable anxiety. We knew he would not be back from America until June. On March 19, all the papers reported his marriage to Joan Plowright, and there were pictures of them dancing down the New York highway after the ceremony. I peered hard at the photos of these two people who would influence my life in the future, trying to discern their characters.

Why did Sir Laurence take on the Chichester project? He explained it in a broadcast in ITV's first edition of *Tempo*, a programme devoted to the Arts. During the interview with Lord Harewood he was seen first of all pacing over the various parts of the half-finished building, soliloquising :—

'This is going to be the theatre they want me to run. Having had two London theatres pulled down round about my ears, it is nice to find myself in one that is going up. Haven't actually run one since they pulled down the old St. James's. A new kind of theatre, this one. What's it going to look like really? What's it going to feel like, with all these faces practically all round? There are a lot of things here . . . new things . . . exciting things. Must be adaptable and for the audience. What's it going to be like all sitting in a ring? Will they worry if they catch sight of Aunt Mabel sitting on the other side of the stage? I suppose the actors will just have to be more interesting to look at. After all, you can see Aunt Mabel at the circus, but most people watch the elephants. Good to be watching it grow like this . . . beautiful . . . awe-inspiring, particularly to me : I am the one who has got to make it work. How many moments of real excitement or real theatre can be provided? What sort of excitement . . . what sort of theatre? First I must decide what sort of plays will suit the theatre, or that the theatre would suit. What about restoration plays, all those 18th century plays? Shakespeare is of course a natural. Molière — but what about Brecht, and what about getting new plays written for this sort of stage? Where does

80

one begin? It will all have to come in time. Anyway, what is a festival? What are they for?'

In a reply to a question about what he really thought festivals were for, he replied that they were to galvanise people's interest in some way or other. 'I suppose they started in religious festival, church festival, spreading to harvest festivals, wine-growing festivals, any trade festival, the old guilds I am sure, the singing festivals, the Eisteddfods, the Meistersingers of Nuremburg bashing away at it, something to make them feel better, something to bring them out of themselves. Something to make them put on their Sunday best to see the best that can be offered to them. Something they would not see otherwise or not be likely to see otherwise.'

When Lord Harewood asked him what made him decide to take on this particular job, to embark on running the Chichester theatre, he replied :—

'Chichester. That was emotional largely. First of all I found it immensely touching in this day and age that perfectly private people could want a thing so badly as the people of Chichester want this theatre. It started, as you know, by Leslie Evershed-Martin, who is an ex-mayor of Chichester, getting together with a few of his cronies ; and they got hold of some influential members of the county and the South of England, and the idea caught fire. When they asked me if I would direct it, I was so touched and so thrilled with the idea of not only just taking this job which has been so voluntarily got together, but also with burning excitement about the theatre itself.'

When asked what he called the building he replied, 'I think it is called an amphitheatre, and I call it that'. When asked if it made any restrictions on the actors, and how he felt about acting on such a stage surrounded on three sides by people, he said :—

'I did it once. I did it by accident. I was playing Hamlet in Elsinore many years ago, and the rain was falling down so hard in the courtyard of the castle where we had to act that it was abandoned and we suddenly had to put it on at no warning at all in the ballroom, and there we found ourselves in just such circumstances. It was very exciting. Here it will be planned, and the star will be the theatre, apart from what goes on inside it; and I hope they will be prodigious, and as King Lear said, "I will do such things — what they are yet I know not, — but they shall be The terrors of the earth." — in a nice way, of course. The stage will be the unifying feature. It is bound to be for the first two or three years, until the people have got used to it and found their way around, and learned to concentrate. I think they will right away, and I think they will concentrate all right. That is the purpose of such a shape — to provide greater concentration on the action.'

When Lord Harewood asked him if he had any distinguishing features for this first Chichester Festival he replied :—

'I am hoping to provide a feast of acting. The hope of my life has been to interest people in acting, to find acting itself interesting to them, and many wonderful things have been said by brains mightier than mine by far. Bernard Shaw called a theatre a temple to be a friend of man. Shelley said the highest thing of drama is the teaching of the human heart the knowledge of itself. I think this is a wonderful opportunity, in which this great art can be shown to better advantage, more interestingly and more excitingly. An actor's theatre, in other words.'

Sir Laurence gave his fee of £500 for this broadcast to the Theatre Building Fund, thereby again demonstrating his generosity to the combined effort.

Chapter Eleven

STONE-LAYING

EARLY IN FEBRUARY 1961 the Duke of Norfolk told me that Princess Alexandra had consented to lay the foundation stone and would also come down to the Eventide Home at Donnington on the outskirts of Chichester, attending the ball in aid of the theatre at Arundel Castle in the evening. This was announced in the Court Circular and on radio on February 14. Preparations for this took up a great deal of time, with memorable visits for me to Kensington Palace to meet the Princess' lady-in-waiting, Lady Moira Hamilton, with whom I discussed the programmes and general arrangements. I enjoyed these visits as much as the ones I had made to Buckingham Palace to arrange for a visit of Her Majesty the Queen to Chichester.

The Board was getting nervous and irritable at this time. We were on the edge of unavoidable decisions. There were surges of petty economies such as whether we needed another model, or a special flag or emblem. The question of a film of the history of the early days was put off endlessly, and in the end was left too late. I had great difficulty in getting them to agree at least to have a band for the foundation stone ceremony, and other, to me, essential commitments for such an occasion.

We were also having a problem with McAlpine regarding the manner in which the payments should be made, and how they could be guaranteed. This went on right up to the Sunday morning ten days before the foundation stone was to be laid. The contractors suddenly altered their requirements, demanding an increased guarantee fund. The scheme was that the guarantors should form a Building Company which guaranteed the regular

83

eight yearly payments, and there was an undertaking by the Trust that all monies paid into it, after a reasonable deduction for promotion expenses (fixed at the maximum of $7\frac{1}{2}$ per cent) must be paid to the Building Company. The Guarantors were Lord Bessborough, Mrs Gestetner, Mr A. T. Smith and Mr Alan Draycott.

This sudden demand for another £10,000 to be guaranteed at the last moment upset us considerably. Building was to have started in a few days' time, and it had been publicly announced that Princess Alexandra would lay the foundation stone. We were in a cleft stick, and we could not postpone without grave results. I spent a very worried day on the telephone to all members of the Trust, who were naturally reluctant to increase their liabilities, having so generously agreed to the large amounts already promised. I knew in my heart that they would certainly be covered, as the rate of donations was increasing ; but this was impossible to prove, and the trustees were nervous. Everything was at stake. It was understandable that, because of the unusually favourable terms they were offering, McAlpine should want full certainty of final payment, but it was a pity they had not stipulated this in the first place. My hair turned greyer that day, as it seemed that everyone was beginning to back away from me. But finally Lord Bessborough rang to say that he would increase his guarantee. His wife, Lady Mary Bessborough, who had always encouraged us all in her delightfully excitable way, decided to add her guarantee to bridge the gap. Here was another instance where people saved the situation and the fact that all these people guaranteed large sums to bring the theatre about should never be forgotten. I shall never forget to be grateful.

But it was a shock that day to realise how easily I could be left isolated. I could never leave this project without public censure — others might be able to do so.

At last the agreements were signed. Within a few days, on May 1, Carol and I were motoring to Brighton, and as we reached the outskirts of Chichester, we saw a huge McAlpine mobile crane parked on the verge. We felt an upsurge of excitement, hoping that this was the beginning of building on the very day promised . . . and it was. When we got back in the evening there

84

was the crane, huts and caravans, on the site and the turf was already being cut.

May 12 was one of those days from heaven that only England can conjure up during a spell of poor weather, and the scene in Oaklands Park was typically Merrie England. Flags on a dozen poles lent by Portsmouth Corporation were quietly fluttering in the breeze, but in front of the flower-bedecked dais was one lonely pole without a flag ; beside the pole a solitary seaman stood at ease waiting for the signal to hoist our own theatre flag, the design of which till then had been kept a secret. The band of the Royal Marines from the Royal Yacht had marched through the city to remind the citizens that this was the day on which they had been invited to join in the celebrations marking the beginning of their theatre. I arranged that every householder got a leaflet with the invitation. There was a large crowd on three sides of a square, but one side was reserved for school children, the elderly, and a polio patient.

Near the dais were special seats for the Trust members and their wives, and a fidgeting line of self-conscious people to be presented. On either side of the dais were the Martlet Swordsmen and Folk Dancers in brilliant costumes of yellow and white completing this very English scene in a typical park. One critic said there was nothing theatrical about it until the ode was spoken at the end, the ceremony being rather formal and civic ; but I felt it should portray the English countryside peopled by the usual dignitaries, with a sudden theatrical touch at the end. We all missed the presence of Sir Laurence and Lady Olivier but they would not be free to return to England until the end of June.

Philip Whitehead had been staff officer to Col. Wingate in the Far East Campaign and he agreed to act as a sort of Master of Ceremonies so that everyone knew where to go and what to do. This he did quietly but with precision, so that all went like clockwork and I did not have to worry. The Board had agreed to invite, through Lord Bessborough, the High Commissioner of Canada, the Rt Hon Mr George Drew, to give the link with Stratford, Ontario. He was one of the first to be introduced to the Princess when she arrived with the Duke of Norfolk from Arundel Castle. As usual, the Duke generously left all the rest of the introductions

85

to Lord Bessborough, having quietly pointed out to us that it was our day and we should have the full enjoyment of being with Her Royal Highness. The Princess captured the hearts of everyone from the moment she arrived to the end of the Arundel Ball at the Castle.

Lord Bessborough welcomed the Princess in a short speech, saying that her gracious act in agreeing to perform the ceremony had set an historic seal upon our endeavours. Philip Powell and Mr W. Cairns, McAlpine's site manager, helped her to lay the foundation stone. In her speech, the Princess said that many theatres in London and the provinces had closed, a fact which could not have escaped the notice of those who initiated this project; she continued 'This is an act of faith and courage on their part which has all our respect and admiration. It is heartening to find so much enthusiasm. May the Festival Theatre meet with every success.' The eight-year-old twins of Alan Draycott presented a bouquet to her, and the Lord Bishop dedicated the site. On behalf of the hundreds of people who had worked so hard and so enthusiastically to create the theatre, I thanked Her Royal Highness for performing the ceremony. I said it was an occasion that would live long in our memories. We had often been labelled 'day-dreamers' but this had been a day beyond our finest dreams.

I also said we believed that public patronage of the Arts was not dead, but responds whole-heartedly when there is a sound but imaginative purpose. People in every income group had joined in this exhilarating endeavour, and that day £50,000 was the total given or promised — more than half the sum required. The Lord Bishop had dedicated the site, and the City Council, under the leadership of the Mayor, had with great foresight leased this piece of ground to the Trust for ninety-nine years at a peppercorn rent. Thus history was repeated when Royalty, Church, the Civic Authority and the People had combined in happy relationship to shape the future. Our good fortune had been abundant but we would have been less than human if we had not had our difficulties. Obviously the story of the past two and a half years would contain a fine mixture of much pleasure and a little pain. I finished by saying that we hear much of harmful radiation in these days, but the radiation of happiness and goodwill as shown by Her Royal

86

Highness, and other members of the Royal family, is an example which, if multiplied throughout the world, would indeed bring peace and understanding. We wished Her Royal Highness, with deep respect, God Speed on her travels in the near future to Hong Kong, Japan, Thailand and Burma, and we hoped we would be honoured with her presence on many future occasions in our theatre.

Teddy Smith, was, at that time, Chairman of Royal Crown Derby, and on behalf of the Trust he presented the Princess with a 42-piece service decorated with hand-painted scenes from Shakespeare and designs of the Chichester Festival Theatre. It was the only one made, and it took three months for the fine engraving to be done by an 80-year-old craftsman, Mr Albert Haddock, the only surviving pupil of the famous ceramic artist Desire Leroy.

Mr Drew then briefly conveyed good wishes from Canada, and when he unfurled the flag of the theatre, which carried the symbol of Minerva, he provided the first theatrical moment of the day.

Here is David Goodman's description of this symbol, designed by one of his colleagues John Newton-Mason :—

'We chose Minerva, the Roman counterpart of Athene, goddess of the arts and sciences and associated with skill, wit and intelligence. Her war connections are perhaps best forgotten in this context. Minerva is depicted in antiquity as a woman in armour ; but with a decidedly masculine physique. She is shown with various symbols, among which the owl appears frequently, and this we liked for its legendary wisdom and because, like the theatre, it is most active in the evening.

The appropriateness of our emblem is, we feel, well established. The theatre itself, though as a building in concrete and glass entirely of this century, has obvious links with the Roman amphitheatre. Moreover, Chichester was an important Roman city as is shown by the celebrated stone, discovered in 1723, and recording the dedication of a temple to Neptune and Minerva.

Our interpretation of the goddess may not delight the pedants. The helmet, for example, has a decidedly Greek character, but it offered more decorative scope than the Roman varieties, and provided an allusion to the arena auditorium. In any event Athene and Minerva are really only slightly differing aspects of the same deity.'

After a fanfare, John Neville stepped in front of the microphone and delivered a sonnet specially composed for the occasion by Christopher Fry, the playwright and poet.

SONNET FOR THE ORATION
by *Christopher Fry*

Shakespeare apologised for having dared
To conjure up within a wooden O
A great conflict of men ; but well he fared
By the imagination's power, so
Transforming an unworthy scaffold to a vast
World, he filled the present with the past.

Now here, in a bare place, with one stone laid,
Suppose our theatre built, you in your places,
In these few halting words a drama played,
And in my face a stage of actors' faces.

Fill the present with the future (a play's toward)
And, for the first of many times, applaud.

Somehow I have always been blessed with brilliant sunshine whenever I have been responsible for special outdoor events ; there has been only one wet day out of fourteen Gala Days ; a storm suddenly lifted when the Queen visited Chichester in 1956 ; and now a lovely day for the laying of the foundation stone of the theatre. Many local people call it E-M's weather. The quotation we had selected for the Arundel Castle souvenir programme rang through my head as Her Royal Highness left for Arundel and we relaxed :-

88

Now, by my faith, Lords, t'was a glorious day ;
And more such days as these to us befall.

The Ball in the evening was a great success financially and socially as it combined for the first time the people from London with those working locally. The main arrangements had been the responsibility of the Sussex members, but the London Committee organised the huge tombola which was the chief means of raising money for the Development Fund. The final total profit from the Ball was £3,500. That the stately Barons Hall was crowded with dancers all the time was due to the excellence of Tim Clayton's band which had been specially requested by the Duke of Norfolk's daughters. Refreshments were good, although the promised early morning bacon and eggs did not materialise in large enough quantities to satisfy the crowd still there. The bars lost money but the caterer insisted on keeping to his bargain and accepted the loss as his contribution. The Princess danced a great deal during the evening and afterwards we were assured from the Palace how much she had enjoyed it all.

Chapter Twelve

REFERENCE BACK TO CANADA

I DECIDED IT was time we saw the theatre at Stratford, Ontario, so Carol and I arranged with Alan and Anne Draycott to meet out there on July 11. They met us at the airport with Mr Victor Polley, general manager of the theatre, his wife, and one of their associates, and we went by car to Stratford. We immediately found there was a common link between Mr Polley and Chichester. His father, as a boy, had been a member of a choir when it visited Chichester Cathedral at a time when Dr. Harvey Grace was the organist. We had left London at midday and so when we got to Stratford it was about midnight to us but only about seven o'clock to them. They took us round by the theatre so that we could get a quick glimpse of it and then on to the theatre president's house. As we drove up, in the cool of a summer evening, we could see a large gathering on the verandah, awaiting our arrival and obviously very curious to see what sort of people we were — this was equalled by our curiosity regarding them.

Several of the Stratford Theatre Trust directors and their wives were present, together with Mr Michael Langham, the artistic director of the theatre, and members of the cast. It was an extremely friendly and merry evening. Neither of us felt the effect of the late hour as the evening went on as we were so stimulated by everything and everybody. At last we were in actual contact with the town and its people whom I had been admiring and talking about for so long. They promised us every possible help, and arrangements were made to entertain us and show us the workings of the theatre during the next six days. The Draycotts and ourselves were not allowed to spend any money at all, as tickets for the theatre and meals with them were all scheduled.

I found Ontario's restrictions on alcohol very difficult when attempting to repay hospitality. We did manage to get to a hotel once and entertain one or two to drinks, but it was all hedged about with regulations. The theatre had been refused licences for bars. I was told by one of the citizens that this came about partly by the intervention of one of the churches, or chapels, regardless of the gesture which had been made the previous year by the theatre to let services and meetings be held in the theatre, for some long time, when a fire had damaged the church.

In the town I was intrigued to guess, each time I met a shopkeeper, whether or not he had been one of those who had opposed the theatre in the early days. None now showed any sign of this when they questioned us as to who we were, and where we came from, and why we were visiting their particular town. They all vowed allegiance to the theatre and spoke of it with pride. Obviously the town was going to prosper from it, though few shopkeepers anywhere in the world admit help in this way. The town needed a boost, as there was a fear that the large railway shunting yards were to be closed. The mournful whistle of the trains was heard very stridently in the theatre in the early days of the tent roof, but it probably linked the town life with the audience in the same way as our Cathedral bells have been heard on Wednesday practice nights : sometimes quite appropriately, as when we were playing *St. Joan* or Ustinov's *Unknown Soldier and his Wife*.

The setting of the park around the Stratford, Ontario theatre, on its slight hill, was splendid. I instantly envied their lake, as expanses of water add so much to the atmosphere of leisure. I dreamed of artificially flooding a section around our theatre, especially as it is a natural watershed, but it was not difficult to imagine the reaction of our planning committee, and it would therefore be better to hope for a fountain one day if a sponsor could be found.

Their dramatic firing of a cannon at the moment when, in conventional proscenium theatres, the curtain would go up was a typical Guthrie inspiration. Remembering the three large

91

hospitals adjacent to our site, it was obvious a cannon would not be acceptable. But perhaps a rocket to burst high in the air with a distant noise and show smoke trails would be an idea. When I returned and mentioned this to Sir Laurence he told me the following tale, and later repeated it in answer to a question from Lord Harewood on *Monitor*, as to whether he had anything personal to Chichester such as a trademark.

'Some years ago Ralph Richardson and I were running the Old Vic and there came a time for us to be married to the National Theatre, to the committee as it existed then. And one day we were walking down a street and Ralph, who is a creature of great imagery, said, 'You know what we will have in our theatre . . . a beautiful idea . . . whenever the curtain goes up each night, there will be a blue rocket ascending into the heaven and the strangers of the town will ask the inhabitants "Please what is that rocket? Do you know? Can you tell me?" "Yes, we can, that is the curtain going up in the National Theatre." So as soon as I took this job I wrote to Ralph and said, "Please can I have your rocket" and he wrote back and said "Of course, you can." So there it is and it shall always be called Ralph's Rocket. A lot of other theatres may borrow the idea most freely but they must always give him due credit.'

Alas, we did extensive research with the firework firms and with several marine and army rocket experts, but there seemed to be no way in which we could overcome the danger of damage to persons and property by the large empty canister when it fell. Bright lights from a rocket would not be seen clearly in daylight, and it would have needed smoke and noise together to attract attention. This meant quite a heavy missile. So Ralph's Rocket was abandoned, through sheer practical impossibility, and this meant another festive idea had gone.

The theatre building at Stratford was imaginatively constructed to follow the pattern of the original tent appearance, but now it contained 2,200 seats instead of the original 1,500. This seemed to me to be a disadvantage in one way, because many hundreds must feel disappointed to find themselves so far from the stage, when they had always understood that the chief idea of the amphitheatre was to keep everyone close around. However, they are still filling the whole theatre for their seasons and making a sensible return on their capital. Wide expanses of glass doors led into a large foyer. They have a Board room and VIP lounge, (which we have still not yet been able to afford), and these were necessary to allow drinks to be offered to special guests in the absence of the bars. The auditorium was impressive, and I thought the only disadvantage was the large balcony separating the audience into two parts. The all-together feeling of our theatre has been cleverly contrived by making the two side balconies sweep out from the centre section, so that people in them feel joined to, and part of, the whole audience.

What of the effect on me of the first play I saw there? I was in a tumult, worrying whether, after all my theorising about the thrust stage, I should be disappointed and would go back to England feeling we had promoted the wrong thing. It would have been disastrous for my peace of mind, as I cared deeply that I should not lead people into a false situation. People may well ask why we had not gone over to Stratford in the first place. We had decided as a Board never to claim any expenses in any way for anything we did for the theatre, so it was just a question of personal economics at the time.

The first play was *Coriolanus* and although I did not care for the production itself, and although it did not seem to fulfil the needs of the stage because the company was smaller than I had expected, I caught the magic of the theatre and felt happy. *Henry VIII* the next night was better, splendidly dressed, with costumes blending with one another — especially in the last scene when everything was gold, pale primrose and buttercup yellow.

The third play, *Love's Labour's Lost*, really brought out the mobility and audience-involvement of the stage. We were absorbed by its beauty. Movement was almost in ballet form, sequence swept into sequence with satisfying continuity. This production showed what really can be done to use all the stage so that those on the sides felt the production was giving them equal presentation to that seen by people in the central seats. There was nothing forced about it, and when the company brought this production to Chichester in 1963 it amazed me how quickly the audience grasped the significance of the Canadians' experienced use of the stage. They were acclaimed, and they are still vividly remembered, not because of any standard of acting, but because of their special ability to use the advantages and conquer the challenges of the thrust stage. As I watched on that third night in Stratford, my hopes for the success of such a theatre with such a stage in the British Isles now became a conviction.

One day, after a long and interesting trip to Niagara Falls, we visited their Avon theatre in Stratford. This was a converted cinema, and used as an auxiliary theatre for musical productions and concerts. We saw Guthrie's version of *The Pirates of Penzance*, and were treated to a rollicking evening. It was full of Guthrie gimmicks, and seemed more like an American musical comedy skit on Gilbert and Sullivan. I imagined the horror with which it would be received in England, where many people look upon it as an almost religious exercise, peering over their scores and shushing at the slightest noise from other members of the audience. It was enjoyable seeing Gilbert and Sullivan treated in this way just for once, but it seemed a waste of Tyrone Guthrie's talents. When he did bring it to England, we saw it at the Theatre Royal, Brighton. He had toned it down for English consumption, but it still caused a lot of hostile criticisms. The local amateur operatic members could hardly trust themselves to speak of it.

Each day Alan Draycott and I investigated all the procedures of box office, accountancy and production costs. They showed us everything; we had full opportunities to put questions to the heads of the various departments. We were given samples of all their stationery and publicity material. I drew up a detailed survey, and it helped us enormously in the very early days before the professionals were fully entrenched at Chichester.

Actually, most box office routines in this country seem to work by antiquated tradition. I especially thought so after I had seen the systems used at the Tyrone Guthrie theatre in Minneapolis when I was there in 1965.

Few theatres can have such spacious facilities as the Stratford, Ontario, theatre. Large rooms, each devoted to one type of costume, such as boots or helmets or armoury, are situated along corridors which lead to the stage like the spokes of a wheel. It was so pleasant meeting Tanya Moisevitch after all we had heard and read about her. Of all the people I have met in the theatre world, I found her one of the most sincere and lovely to talk to. She was the inspiration there in devising the setting of the stage, with its many balconies and jigsaw island acting spaces, besides the designing of so many of their plays.

Alan Draycott was not so interested in details of theatre procedures, box office routines, etc., as in the financial implications of the productions and balance sheets. He concentrated on people who could tell him of profit and loss, and he triumphantly came up with the gift the Stratford people made of all the maple wood required to make our stage. This was a splendid and generous gesture; eventually the wood arrived in Chichester and was made into our stage. They had used English oak for their stage and the maple was symbolic of the friendship which had arisen from our following their lead in a theatre of this kind. When they came to Chichester with their company in 1963, I enjoyed making a personal gift to them of a silver loving cup to seal further the bond.

After two days the Draycotts left to return to England, but we stayed on and had the opportunity, at last, to entertain a good number of the theatre people to dinner at the Country Club restaurant. But I had to bludgeon them, and pretend to consider it an insult if they did not accept. They were so generous, they wanted to do the entertaining all the time. It was a vivid lesson to remember when we had people from other countries coming to see our theatre in the future.

I was embarrassed when two or three of the publicity and wardrobe personnel approached me regarding possibilities of their being engaged for Chichester, and I immediately said that I was not talent-spotting. In fact, nothing had been further from my mind, and I could not think of abusing my position as guest. I stipulated that if they discussed their future with Mr Polley, and the Stratford Theatre did not want to retain their services, or if their reasons were sympathetically understood, only then would I consider their proposals — in the presence of Mr Polley.

The Stratford administration told me that in the case of Mr Ivan Alderman, head of the wardrobe department, they had known for a year or so that he wished to return to England and they would quite understand if I negotiated with him. He was one of the finest appointments we ever made. Recognised as the most talented cutter of men's wardrobe in the theatre world, he was the inspiration of our wardrobe department. We were sorry to lose him to the National Theatre later on.

Carol and I moved on after six exhilarating days in Stratford and visited friends in Chicago and Philadelphia. In the latter city we saw a performance in 'The Theatre in the Park' created there by the father of Grace Kelly, Princess of Monaco. It was a pleasant experience of a small theatre in-the-round with an almost circus atmosphere. The play was weak but the production in the round was good.

After returning home in the *Mauretania*, I was able to reassure our Board that I had no regrets about our decision to have such a theatre as we had planned. Alan Draycott also confirmed his belief in it, having now seen the possibilities. So we got back to the parochial worries of getting the building finished and preparing for the opening.

Chapter Thirteen

BUSINESS TEMPERS AND THEATRICAL TEMPERAMENTS

ON JUNE 23 I met Sir Laurence and Joan Plowright for the first time. They arrived at my consulting rooms at about five in the evening. We stood for a few minutes talking and appraising one another by using the normal opening gambits. Without ever having met, we had committed ourselves, from afar, to work together for at least a year. They had, of course, met Lord Bessborough, but a lot of happiness depended on the atmosphere which would surround their contacts with me and the other members of the Board. Now they searched my eyes and I for my part analysed them for all I was worth. I was happy at this first meeting.

In the following years, Olivier and I had many tussles, mainly because although we both wanted an uncompromising agreement on standards for our theatre, which were not always hallowed in other theatres, he had a healthy distrust of the opinion of anyone who did not depend on the theatre for a living. Every suggestion I made was met by a wary look, a stepping-back attitude and long pauses for thought. This expression is perfectly caught in the portrait I have of him painted by Bernard Hailstone.

I shall never forget the occasion when he produced some 'do's and dont's' for the audience, to be printed in the programme. As an ordinary member of the audience I should have been rebuffed and annoyed by some of these, and would have felt that my intelligence had been under-rated. With some of them I was frankly horrified! His attitude was a natural one; being a great artiste, he was nervous, especially in an amphitheatre, that acting would be ruined by the inconsiderate late comer, the cougher, the chocolate box rattler or by the provincial tendency to applaud entrances, exits and telling lines.

We sat, side by side, in his dressing room, which for the first year he had to use as an office, and I gave my reasons why I hoped he would drop the idea, or at least make extensive alterations. He sat still and pensive for five or more minutes without saying a word. Although the silence seemed to last hours, I knew this was a trial of strength which I could not afford entirely to lose : so I remained silent, too, determined not to be the next to speak, after having already made all my points. Eventually the deathly quiet was broken ; although he was annoyed with me, I know he enjoyed the drama of it. He was deliberately inflicting this punishment on me for my audacity, in his opinion, in disagreeing with a professional. I have the same healthy distrust of experts in all walks of life as he has of non-theatrical people. He made some concessions on wording and took the sting out of the worst parts, so I eventually thought the following would be more acceptable.

The compromise document read :-

THEATRE NOTES

'May we express to you, our audience, our great pleasure in your company and our heartiest welcome to this theatre, the whole design of which is a bid for communication in a world in which the lack of it is the ostensible source of so much complaint and disappointment. Exchange of emotion, whether conveyed in laughter, sympathy or silent understanding, is the communion through which the theatre may live and breathe.

As some of our audience may be newcomers to the medium, it is respectfully suggested that owing to the nature of the theatre, disturbances of any kind are a great distraction and even that such applause as they feel generously prompted to give would be more than ever welcome if confined to the ends of the acts, or the play.

There will be an interval of 18 minutes. The co-operation of our audience is most earnestly requested in returning to their seats in ample time for the continuation of the performance, as delay in this will result in their inconvenience.

Owing to the nature of the theatre and the production, the entrances of both actors and audience are frequently the same, so that after the start of the action such entrances must, of necessity, be closed to the public.

As smoking in the auditorium makes life intolerable for both spectators and performers, and as the Fire Department have decided that it makes life intolerable for them, too, that, we are afraid, is that.

Another occasion was when there had been a Royal visit and we were all exhausted after the pleasurable excitements and responsibilities this had caused. I returned to the stage and found Sir Laurence and Laurier Lister standing there alone and looking at the empty theatre. It was at this moment that Sir Laurence told me that he intended to revive *Uncle Vanya* the next year. I was naturally shocked, as I had been looking forward to hearing that we should have three different plays each season. I protested that I had thought we would be going forward and not backward. I had always been the champion of the principle that the Director should have freedom regarding the artistic choice and direction of the plays, but this did not mean that we should not be able to comment on his selection. It was always his right to decide eventually. He obviously disliked the fact that I had not hailed his idea as a good one and he proceeded to say something which I found very hurtful at the time.

Next day, he apologised for what he had said and I gladly accepted this, telling him that of course he must do whatever he wished for next year. It was one of those incidents which are bound to occur between men working together on something about which they both feel deeply. We were soon back to our former friendly relationship . . . one which has existed ever since. As everyone now knows I was completely wrong in my judgement, as the *Vanya* production was an even greater success the next year.

Most contentions were between the two of us as in most cases the other members of the Board did not feel so deeply about matters which I considered important. However, our relationship moved into an atmosphere of greater respect for each other as time went on. The wounds were slight and soon healed. For all his pretence, at times, to appear otherwise Sir Laurence is a man with a deep conscience and of sterling integrity. I knew that whenever he had said or done things which were mischievously hurtful or insincere, he would, for certain, be on the telephone next morning expressing his regrets. I can work with any man who has a conscience, whatever differences we might have but if there is no basic quality or a firm belief in what is right and what is wrong, it is hopeless. I only hope I responded as well as he did when I was wrong.

Apart from these normal clashes of temperament that were bound to occur, Carol and I enjoyed to the full his warm and colourful nature. It was, and still is, always a delight to meet him or hear his voice on the telephone. He never failed to show his interest in us both and in our family affairs. The proof of our pleasure in having known him is that we enjoy having his portrait looking down on us every day in our lounge.

His devotion to perfection in his art was revealed in many ways while he was with us. I soon learned that his change of mood, his alterations in approach and manner of speech, would be revealed in the next part he created. He had been practising on us all the time! That different lift of an eyebrow, the long slow lick of the lips done in a new way, or the throwing of the head with an upward glance in a more accelerated or reduced timing were all meaningful. I made it a rule never to watch rehearsals unless I was invited. I fully appreciated the slight stiffening that would come when 'there is a stranger in the house'. But he often invited me with a friendly 'Even if I allow no one else, Leslie, surely you of all people should be able to come and watch.' I was careful to sit obscurely at the back, but he would still seek me out and chat, or introduce me to someone.

As we moved into 1962, meetings became more difficult. Everyone was getting more on edge about the running of the theatre. Pieter Rogers, who was general manager of the Royal Court, had been introduced to me by Elspeth Cochrane in May before Sir Laurence had arrived on the scene. I realised at once that he would be a brilliant head of our administration, but left the decison until Sir Laurence could make his own arrangements. He immediately agreed. Pieter Rogers was a very volatile personality, and was not easy to work with at times because he changed in mood and direction as a chameleon changes colour. We were as different as chalk and cheese, but running through the many turbulent times there was an appreciation of each other's particular qualities. He had a fantastic memory for everything about the theatre and could tell you accurately, if a little caustically, every play, with dates, and places, which any actor or actress had ever been in. I always felt that one of the reasons our small parts were played so well in the early days was due to his help in casting them. Staffs working under him were always loyal except in one or two cases of members becoming exasperated because he wanted to do their work for them, often because he could in fact have done it better.

The Board had been the most marvellous group of people to raise funds for the building. None could have excelled them in this. But they felt they needed reinforcement when it came to real theatre problems, and some of them wanted someone on the Board who was expert in theatre matters. They had soon forgotten that the whole of the detailed plan I had conceived, even before I met Tyrone Guthrie, had in fact worked out exactly and correctly, even if I had been unusually lucky with it. They were all people who were engaged in big business, and they believed that anyone engaged in a professional way of life did not understand finance. This was probably true when it came to intricate company matters, but as regards theatre matters I had always listened to all the expert advice I could get. I suppose some people might have reconstituted the Board when the money had been raised, but it was not in me to drop anyone who had helped to make it all possible. So we carried on, and I fought the battles as they came.

I was quite sure that Sir Laurence would not agree to another member of his profession sitting on the Board, and he would have shied away from discussions on theatrical matters. All actors, I found, changed their attitude when a lay person entered their gatherings. I also noticed that one actor immediately put up a professional guard when he hears another laying down the law about the theatre. This happens with all experts in all professions. I always argued that while we could always seek professional opinion, as I had been able to do freely from the beginning, once there was a professional on the Board he would assume the mantle of authority. The lay people would tend to accept his ruling as the view of theatre people, and yet he could be completely wrong, since so many differences of opinion can be found on theatrical problems.

When we appointed a director, he alone should be the authority and we must abide by his artistic direction. He should, of course, in all reason, hear the views of the public, as represented by the Board, on such matters as priority bookings, price of seats, effect of publicity, first night procedures and public relations with the authorities and townsfolk.

The great differences between the creation of our theatre and most commercial theatres was that the public themselves were building it. Everyone who had given money had a tremendous personal interest in its running and its success. The personal demands on the box office alone were extremely unusual, especially with a large Society priority booking. Money must be spent locally as much as possible. Behaviour of everyone working in the theatre should blend with the local people with whom they were lodging. There was the noise factor to be considered because of the adjacent hospitals, and tactful negotiation was needed with the local football club to damp down their loudspeaker. Their pitch was very near, and half-time announcements could have devastting effects on a Saturday matinée play.

All in all, the Board, Sir Laurence and the management were difficult elements to weld together, but it says much for everyone's devotion to the scheme that we got through these very trying days up to the opening without a break. The skirmishes, or battles, were bloodless, soon settled without rancour. Everyone was determined that everything should be done in the best possible way according to their sincere convictions. Many people, especially the members of the Board, were individualists who had made successes of their lives. That was why they were on the Board, and they would have been less than human if they had not at times displayed these characteristics. Now after many years the members of the Board work in great harmony, confident and experienced.

Chapter Fourteen

NEAR HOME AND NEAR DISASTER

FROM THE DAY the building started, it was difficult to keep away from the site. McAlpine appointed a first class site manager, Mr W. Cairns, to take charge of the whole job, and he was determined to complete the work successfully on time. He stood no nonsense with casual labour or sub-contractors. Nothing was allowed to delay progress and if a crane or other machine broke down, there was a replacement immediately on its way from London. The whole operation was magnificently timed throughout and there were no difficulties with the local authorities because of the care and attention paid by the contractors to the surrounding parkland.

We were lucky to have such a firm with such resources who were willing to build what was to them a minor building, but one which they realised had prestige in its uniqueness and national interest. Their motto, I understand, is that every day they are on a site longer than necessary is money lost to them. They also knew our anxiety and need for perfect timing. Unlike a factory or block of flats which can be delayed without very serious consequences for a few weeks, a theatre had to be ready in full time for rehearsals to begin a definite number of weeks before the opening. Any delay on the starting date of rehearsals meant a postponement of the opening night, with all the catastrophe of returned tickets and broken contracts with the actors. It would be unthinkable.

Week by week the building rose rapidly and visiting the site became a local pilgrimage for the populace, especially on Saturdays and Sundays. Architects and building operatives were constantly asking permission to watch the various stages, as many intriguing new concepts of engineering and construction were being used. Many TV interviews took place with Sir Laurence, Lord Bessborough and myself in the skeleton of the building and commentators strode the foundations of the stage mouthing Shakespeare quotations to introduce or end their documentaries.

I was determined not to lose any opportunity of thanking and encouraging the site manager and workers. The chance came at the topping out ceremony on November 23 when the theatre flag was flying to indicate that the highest point of the building had been reached. Most of us climbed the perilous ladders to the top staging under the skeleton roof with Sir Laurence, to meet Mr Cairns and the workmen gathered there. Olivier was soon at home with them joking about the beer that was there and demanding to know why they were not getting on with their work. After a quick introduction by me, Sir Laurence congratulated them on the speed with which the building was going up and the interest they were all taking in its final appearance. He won their hearts by wishing he could take them all back with him to Brighton to finish off the alterations to his house, which were already delayed several months. They would have followed him anywhere. The well-known BBC commentator, Martin Muncaster, who was taking a special interest in our theatre, managed to interview Sir Laurence high up in the roof and this proved a very successful broadcast next day.

On December 6 members of the Arts Council accepted an invitation to see the progress of the building, examine the plans and scheme, and meet members of the Board. Sir Laurence was filming at the time and could not be with us. The Chairman, Lord Cottesloe, the Secretary-General, Sir William Emrys Williams, Mr Hodgkinson and one or two others came, and as they left to catch the train back to London each one congratulated us. They said what an enjoyable day it had been for them, and remarked that it was pleasant not to be pressed by harassed people for large grants, because we were seeking the money direct from the public.

Alongside the new Trust and Production Companies I had, so far, retained the General Committee that had been with me originally. But the organisation had now became unwieldy, and reluctantly we agreed to disband it. I was sorry to lose the help of so many of the early stalwarts, but after careful explanations they understood. Nearly all of them were incorporated as trustees, or else they helped the various fund-raising committees.

It would be tedious to recount the scores of fund raising efforts, the lectures and interviews that took place in the months preceding the opening. Suffice to say that the tempo increased, with everyone working furiously hard to get the money, and in making decisions in co-operation with Sir Laurence and the management on every conceivable aspect of policy; in addition all of us were running our own businesses every day.

On January 10, 1962, Sir Laurence announced the date of opening as July 5, for a nine week season. The plays were to be *The Chances*, a comedy by John Fletcher, *The Broken Heart* by John Ford and *Uncle Vanya* by Anton Chekhov. The casts were to include Sir Lewis Casson, Fay Compton, Joan Greenwood, Nicholas Hannen, Kathleen Harrison, Keith Michell, John Neville, Sir Laurence Olivier, Joan Plowright, Sir Michael Redgrave, Athene Seyler and Dame Sybil Thorndike.

The news stunned the theatre world, especially when Olivier announced that he would direct all three plays and act in the last two. I was excited beyond words that indeed we were getting not just the best but so much of the best! The news was in nearly every paper of repute and the critics, both drama and local ones, sat back and waited.

In March, at the excellent suggestion of Philip White-head, we decided to rent the *Unicorn* Hotel, at the East Gate of Chichester, for wardrobe and rehearsal purposes. These hotel premises, which had been empty for a year or so, were on a prominent peninsular site, and at one time had been a focal point for the Tangmere Battle of Britain pilots, and scores of their signed photos had been on display in the bars. Now the oval ballroom, where so many Chichester functions had been held, was desolate. It soon became peopled by Ivan Alderman and a friendly wardrobe department in what seemed to be a perpetual earthquake area. Directly you entered you could tell whether or not there was a crisis on hand. If there was, people spoke singly, in clipped sentences. If not, everybody happily talked at once.

Despite all the difficulties they had to overcome, their own temperaments, and those of designers, directors, actors and actresses, they always welcomed us and we found ourselves enjoying all their personalities. Ivan Alderman's interpretation of the materials used and the actual styles of cutting endowed the costumes with a finish and brilliance that even the designers could not have expected. Such excellence was, and is, so necessary for the closeness of the thrust stage. Shabby, patched or unlaundered material cannot be concealed, but his art in having materials sprayed to give a higher gloss or sheen could enhance a cheaper material and make it look more luxurious. The result was costumes of superb elegance. Our family still enjoy the friendship of Ivan Alderman and many of the original department who are still with him at the National Theatre, where they moved on with Sir Laurence.

On May 3 the theatre building was finished, about a week before completion was due. Teddy Smith handed over the building to the Trust from the Building Committee at a cost of £105,000. We all sighed with relief that it was complete and ready for the furnishings and carpets to go straight in. We had been forced to reconsider our ideas regarding tents for restaurants, as the licensing authorities, while allowing licences for events of about a week's duration, such as agricultural shows or races, would not do so for two months. It therefore meant a temporary building for a restaurant and another for offices. Luckily the city Planning Committee agreed to these, but it meant an extra cost of £12,000. However, we could already count on £102,000 so we were getting near the total amount. It seemed that we were in for a quieter time from the point of view of worry . . . but never trust a lull !

On May 29, just five weeks away from opening night and with rehearsals in full swing, we applied to the local magistrates for a theatre licence. The local authorities, and especially the fire officer, had been consulted at every turn, and agreement had been reached on all points. We understood that everything had been done to obey the fire regulations and to consult all the authorities. Apparently it would have been more tactful to consult with the local magistrates and seek their view before we officially applied to the Bench for a licence.

We were dismayed when they suggested the fire precautions were inadequate. The difficulty arose because no licensing authority in the area had any experience in dealing with new theatres and certainly no one in the British Isles had any experience of the kind of auditorium stage which had no proscenium or safety curtain. Obviously it was absurd to impose the normal sort of GLC regulations to a theatre like this. Gangways were wide and there were a great many exits. The building, except for the roof, was entirely of concrete and the seat coverings and carpets were of nylon which would melt and not burn. All exits led down to the foyer which was large and wide at all points and with a great many doors leading straight out to the Park and level with it. There were none of the long winding corridors and flights of steps from considerable heights that are such fire traps in the older theatres.

We had already given up the idea of a fireproofed carpet in the foyer at the behest of the fire authorities. They had insisted on a ventilating system which had to work against convection by drawing all the air under the stage, or at the side of it, instead of being able to take it away in the roof with hot air rising naturally. It was reasonable to prevent any back stage smoke from being drawn into the auditorium but few people realised this when they criticised the air conditioning of our theatre, for this was our most acute problem. Obviously we should have full refrigerating air conditioning when we put heating in the theatre in the next phases.

We had bent over backwards to meet all the requirements imposed and understood that it was all accepted, but the Bench felt they could not approve the licence. The greatest difficulty with fire precautions is that once someone has pointed out a possible hazard, no matter how trivial and improbable it might be, it lays everyone open to charges of criminal negligence if the remedy is not adopted after being recommended.

Urgent discussions took place next day when a list of 15 requirements was ordered to be finished for the magistrates to inspect on June 25 before the formal application next day (the 26th) with our opening night one week later. We were left with less than three weeks to complete the work; the theatre was in turmoil with rehearsals; we faced the threat that if only 99 per cent of the requirements were met at the inspection we should not get the licence and could not open. While some of the items were constructive many were trivial, but there was no time for detailed argument. We decided the best way was to make absolutely certain that everything was done.

Luckily this sort of campaign was right up the street for the energy, 'know-how' and commanding spirit of Jim Battersby and he got down to it with relish. Within a day or two everything was in motion. Miracles were made to happen, contractors and workmen tore into it at his behest.

Even Sir Laurence understood and put up with the chaos of noise during rehearsals ; and we realised the slightest noise is the unforgivable sin for any theatre to inflict on the actors. We were all in the same boat and if we did not pull together we would be sunk. Rails had to be driven into concrete, fixtures altered and every bit of paint in the foyer altered to be more fire-resisting than specified before, even though most of it was attached flat on concrete and would be very difficult to burn. Some of the requirements were due to a misconception of the new requirements of a modern building such as ours, which could hardly be equalled for safety. We did not mind so much the extra cost of several thousands of pounds nor would we resist any of the requirements, but the method and timing of the embargo irked us.

We were deeply concerned that when all was said and done there could easily have been fresh demands at the final hearing or in the meantime comments might appear in print somewhere casting doubts on the safety of the fire prevention arrangements which would have been extremely unjust and would have done us irreparable harm. By agreement I took legal advice with David Biart. He was now our legal adviser, he had done splendid work as Secretary of the companies and had drawn up their complicated constitutions. We briefed a QC to appear for us at the licensing court. I also thoroughly investigated the possibility of turning the theatre into a club for whatever number of weeks were necessary (an appeal would have taken some time). Everyone who had booked tickets (and we were heavily booked for the first play) would have been enrolled as a member after the usual formalities.

Jim Battersby, however, achieved the impossible and on June 25 we solemnly walked round the building with some of the magistrates. Every detail of the 15 requirements was minutely examined and found to be correct. I arrived on the scene just after the introductions had been made and was somewhat surprised to find a bearded man in rather old-fashioned clothes walking round with me. I supposed he was one of the recently appointed magistrates I had not met previously. When, however, he made some caustic asides to me and gave me a wink I suddenly realised it was Sir Laurence Olivier dressed for his part as the doctor, Mihail Lvovitch in *Uncle Vanya*. It was typical of his constant search for perfection that he lived in his costumes around the theatre.

The next day we were still nervous of a possible further delay to the granting of the licence and were all assembled, with our QC, amongst confident publicans seeking extensions to licences for wedding receptions and dances, harassed motorists wondering about the endorsement of their licences and a few petty offenders. None of their worries seemed to compare to ours but after one formal question our licence was granted. We were free to open. To be fair we could not blame the magistrates. They could always justify their opinion that the precautions left absolutely nothing to chance. The fault was on our side that we had not known of the necessity of letting the magistrates see the plans and get their comments before applying for the licence. The old Army adage about reconnaissance should have been remembered.

One amusing outcome was the 'battle of the roses' that had taken place over a mound designed at one corner of the theatre site by the architects as an artistic feature. There had been serious discussions about the look of the grass-covered, flint-walled rather nondescript mound. At least it seemed nondescript to us and I had urged rose trees as being better to crown it with than grass. The architects stuck their heels in and would not agree so we had reached deadlock. With the new fire requirements we were ordered to remove it completely as a hazard, so the battle was over.

During all this time the actors had been arriving in the city and lodgings, cottages and houses had been found for them according to rank. There was the usual musical chairs happenings when some became temperamental over the places chosen for them, but they soon settled down and began to add colour and interest to the life of the city.

On Sunday, June 3, we had the Festival Theatre Evensong Service at the Cathedral. Pieter Rogers and I had been working on this with the Dean and the Archdeacon for some time. The members of the Chapter were very pleased with the idea of starting the Festival with a link with the Cathedral.

It was another very sunny day, and we waited outside the West door, anxiously hoping the Commonwealth Youth procession would leave their service in time for ours at 4 p.m. When they left, Carol and I entered with the Bessboroughs. I was astounded, and very moved, to find the Cathedral packed, with scores of extra seats being hurriedly placed down both sides. It was truly wonderful to see such a large congregation. The Oliviers were in the front pew, looking pleased to be with us, and most of the cast had come as well. Some of the junior members, late arrivals, were looking bewildered, searching for seats and getting in anywhere as the impressive procession of choir and clergy advanced up the aisle. It was a splendid and memorable service and the singing by the Cathedral choir, despite some peeping by the choirboys to spot the stars, was of the very high standard which John Birch, the Cathedral organist and honorary music adviser to the theatre, has created.

The congregation sang the hymns with enthusiasm, but I just wanted to listen and savour to the full this great sound of praise and thanksgiving for all the blessings we had received. The Bishop, Dr Roger Wilson, preached a sermon which portrayed his true sincerity and deep interest in the theatre and its meaning in the lives of everyone. Afterwards, when he and Mrs Wilson entertained the cast and members of the Trust in the heraldic ceilinged dining room in the Palace, he gave further evidence of his friendliness and his concern to know the people who would be with us during this first historic season.

I would have liked a short service of dedication in the theatre the following day, but I took Pieter Rogers' advice that this might be imposing on the members of the cast and management, as they were not all of the same religion but had well supported the Cathedral service. I think the service had been far more realistic in present day circumstances than Guthrie's dream of a great ecclesiastical procession winding through the streets of Chichester.

When the Dean and I discussed the matter of another Cathedral service the following year, we came to the conclusion that it would not be a good idea to have an annual service because as the years went by it might lose its significance, and not be well attended. Perhaps we might have one in 1971 as a special commemoration of the first ten seasons.

The next day, June 4, we met the cast in the foyer for coffee, before they started their rehearsals there and at the Minerva studios. Sir Laurence told the actors about the theatre and the Trust and welcomed them to Chichester. This was a gay affair, and it immediately established a co-operation between us which was to increase during the following months. I told them we had aimed at the stars, but had never expected the whole firmament. From then on I was enthralled to see the whole place alive, dressing rooms littered with costumes and personal belongings, odd corners of the foyer being used to paint last minute additions to props and scenery, heated discussions taking place under the stage or over at the offices and autograph hunters already on the prowl for victims. Stars of international repute strolled through the city getting to know the shopkeepers, who in their turn boasted of their friendship with them.

I spent several days with Peter Maggs and John Boorman of the BBC who were filming an hour-long documentary on the creation of the theatre. They called it *Concrete Vision*. Our house almost became a TV studio. This film was shown on the night we opened, so none of us saw it broadcast but the BBC very kindly presented me with a copy of it. It is a piece of history to keep, and enjoy, since it portrayed so many of the people and incidents I have described in this account.

Southern ITV also made a film which was shown late the first night and we did see some of that broadcast. They had spent an hour trying to take shots of me walking along the Cathedral promenade and from the City Cross to the theatre shop. Whereas the traffic had been sparse before they started it perversely became dense whilst they were filming and I was greatly embarrassed when an indulgent policeman on point duty held up the traffic for them. During one shot two schoolgirls from Brockenhurst asked me for my autograph. Fame at last, I thought, but they looked disappointed when they read my signature, saying they thought I was Andre Morrell. They did cheer up a little when I told them I had thought out the idea of the theatre for they had been sent to Chichester to do an essay on it. The cameras waited patiently. Just as they were whirring again a most exotic lady, in her seventies, henna-dyed hair, plastered face, blue slacks and buttercup yellow low cut blouse, came up to ask me the way to the Post Office. I was praying all the time that the cameras had stopped, as a TV showing of that incident would have killed my reputation in Chichester for good. The cameramen were discreet; they did not know what she had said to me, but they nearly expired when during the next shot a woman shopper upset her trolley basket, all her goods were scattered around me and I was helping to pick them up for her.

Our Mayor, Councillor Selsby, really appreciated the advent of the theatre during his term of office and to celebrate the fact he held a garden party in Priory Park for the entertainment of the cast, management and Production Board. It was a very pleasant evening, with the RAF band playing and was the first social occasion of the season. Pleased by this gesture, everyone turned up from the theatre to meet some of the prominent citizens.

Chapter Fifteen

HOME AND DRY

AT LAST CAME July 5, the opening night of the Chichester Festival Theatre. We were 'home and dry' with the full amount of £110,000 collected in cash or grossed up convenants. Free of all debt on the building and furnishing we had enough money in the box office to cover the guarantees we had all given for the running of the first productions, and there were only a few thousands to find for the restaurant and office buildings.

Everything was ready as I strolled around that morning. I was surprised at the lack of apparent last minute preparation that I thought would be a feature of a theatrical enterprise. It said much for the work of Sir Laurence and Pieter Rogers that, despite the extraordinary difficulties, all was now in order and there was a quiet confidence, at least on the surface, following the hectic dress rehearsals.

Whilst many of my ideas to make the area festive had gone, such as street decorations, a dozen or more flag poles around the car park and entrances, a wine and cheese bar in the foyer selling the English wine from the Hambledon vineyard owned by Sir Guy Salisbury-Jones nearby in Hampshire, benches and tables for picnics, still I was pleased that we had not fallen into the usual rut of restaurants. We had the tremendous luck to get in touch with David Enders and John Glen who owned the exclusive L'Aiglon restaurant in Chelsea. They evolved the idea of having smörbröd meals in the true Danish style. They brought an inspired chef named Jens Have over from Denmark and the meals were a great success. It took the first year for people to understand what it was all about but those who were used to dining out as compared with those seeking the usual three-course under-ten-shillings meal, soon filled the Restaurant before and after the performances. Enders and Glen were both well known for many stage and TV appearances and they soon created a unique atmosphere of genuine friendliness combined with the gaiety of a theatre night-out. They had an uncanny skill in finding and selecting some of the most pleasant girls as waitresses that could be found anywhere, under the direction of Lady May Whitley, well known in BBC circles, and this is a feature that is most appreciated by their patrons.

After my stroll everything began to speed up and it became a dizzy race to keep up with the headlong pace as the hours hurtled by. Telegrams of good wishes poured in from friends far and near, besides those from other theatres like Stratford, Ontario. Flowers arrived for Carol from the Chichester Festival Theatre Society, the Inner Wheel members and other friends. Sir Laurence, warm hearted and generous as ever, sent her the most gorgeous basket of orchids and roses. We sent Joan Plowright a bouquet of 'Carol' roses, and on future occasions, whenever we did this, Sir Laurence wore one in his buttonhole in the play. The Board had also prepared a small present for each member of the cast, to appear on their dressing tables with a personal letter from me as Chairman.

Crowds began to assemble. Once again my weather luck had turned up trumps. TV cameras were everywhere. Although I had received a letter earlier from Mr Moss of Moss Bros regretting that we had not stipulated evening dress for all performances, as at Glyndebourne, it has been the custom always on first nights for quite a fair proportion of men to wear dinner jackets. To promote this for ordinary nights would have spoilt the cosmopolitan cross-section of the public which always come to the theatre. On this night there was some splendid dressing by the ladies. Carol looked gloriously happy and lovely. David and Barry looked tremendously excited. It was indeed a night that will never be equalled for this theatre.

We had received something like three times the number of applications for the 1,350 seats available and allotting them had been a dreadful and heartbreaking task. After an allocation of seats to the Press, friends or members of the cast not in *The Chances*, and those for the Board and Founder members, there had to be a ballot amongst the members of the Society for the rest. There were many heartburnings amongst those who did not get tickets, especially if they had helped a great deal; but you cannot get three people in every seat. The drama critics from every national and local newspaper and representatives from world wide agencies were there because of Sir Laurence and because of this new style of theatre for England. A group of Japanese newsmen flew to England just for the one night. Our first heavily-loaded London train for the theatre somewhat startled the normally phlegmatic railway staff and taxi drivers.

At four minutes to seven Sir Laurence's taped voice boomed out from the loudspeakers. He was counting the audience down in most pleasant and persuasive tones asking them to be seated. It was as though this Cathedral city had adopted the Muezzin's call to prayer from a minaret; or perhaps it was like a moon rocket being counted down to blast-off as he said 'The performance will commence in four minutes'. Interesting, different and as unique as I had wanted everything to be with this theatre; but the real rocket . . . Ralph's Rocket . . . would have been more fun. I had even tried to get Mounties from Canada but this was tabooed by the moods of small economies the Board kept on having. In the same way they rejected my idea of the traditional silk programmes for the first night. If we had used Sekers silks it would have made a pleasant link with one of our trustees, Sir Nicholas Sekers, and his beautful theatre in Cumberland.

What a tremendous thrill my family and I had as we went to our seats, in the fifth row, the ones we always occupy. We looked round at a vast sea of faces all excited and happy with expectation of the commencement of this gala night. If only time was not rushing along so fast so that I had no time to savour each moment. It was suddenly all worth while to be there with scores of friends unknown to me three years ago. One only needed to remember the host of people who had caught the spirit of the adventure and helped so loyally; many times had they sunk their pride to ask for the money to make it possible. Goodwill had been abundant, proving once again that the pioneering spirit still exists in

Great Britain whenever it is not flattened by bureaucracy.

On that first night we paid for all our seats, and we have never had a free seat in the theatre ever since. We made a pact in the Board that we should all do this, and to this day no member of the Board has had anything free. We felt that once that sort of thing began there would be no end to it. Several years later, on the liner *France* returning from New York, I happened to mention this fact to the managing director of a large British firm. He immediately offered a covenant for the theatre which resulted in over £500 to the development fund.

At 7.15 p.m. we had the following telegram sent to Her Majesty the Queen.

'As the first actor steps on to the stage of this new Chichester Festival Theatre, the Trustees, the Board of Management and the Company send loyal greetings to Your Majesty and Prince Philip and look forward to your gracious presence on July thirty-first'.

signed BESSBOROUGH

L. EVERSHED-MARTIN

LAURENCE OLIVIER

At 9.15 p.m. a telegram was sent from her Majesty to Lord Bessborough at the theatre thanking everyone for the kind message of loyal greetings.

At 7. p.m. the National Anthem sounded, and the theatre began to live.

The first play that season, *The Chances*, was a gay romp from beginning to end. I leave the description of it to the newspaper files. I enjoyed it, but I cannot say I relaxed to it, being far too sensitive to the running of the theatre, wanting it to be one hundred per cent perfect. It has taken a few years for me to be able to sit back and forget all else but the play. There are the latecomers, with the particular problems they present in such a theatre, where the slightest movement can be seen out of the corner of the eye. Then there is the behaviour of the attendants, and the ventilation difficulties sometimes causing people to fan themselves with their programmes. There were the whiplash crackings in the roof that

116

puzzled us and annoyed us for a long time, until we found they were caused by the roof rods biting into edges of the concrete and scraping every time there were sudden changes of temperature. Items like these would not concern other people who did not feel responsible for the theatre's reputation. I can easily get absorbed and live completely in a play when it is well acted in any other theatre, but in this one, though I see most productions two or three times, I cannot escape these preoccupations.

When the play ended there was a tremendous ovation stimulated by sentiment and a release from tension as much as by the play itself. We had agreed that the first night of the theatre should be no different in its impact from any other and so there were no ceremonies and no speeches. Christopher Fry most generously wrote a prologue for the evening to complete the poetic link he had created with the theatre at the stone-laying. But Sir Laurence had to decide reluctantly that he could not possibly weave anything into the first night happening without breaking the dramatic force of a purely theatrical first night. Either in costume . . . and he was not acting in the first play . . . or in ordinary clothes it would be incongruous for him to appear before the type of play he was presenting. The prologue was, however, printed in the programmes and we were deeply grateful to Christopher Fry for understanding the difficulty.

PROLOGUE

FOR

CHICHESTER FESTIVAL THEATRE

A theatre speaking for the age
We live in, has an ancient need :
The link between audience and stage
For which I come to intercede.

Long ago in this old city
The Romans met, as you today
To share the laughter, fear and pity,
On summer evenings, listening to a play.

Though now we know a great unrest
Men of another world almost
The mortal heart is still the guest,
The human story still the host.

This is my welcome to you, here
In a place where generations went
To whirl away time at the Sloe Fair,
Not far from where we have pitched our concrete tent.

Under the sign of Minerva, she
Of the old wisdom, we shall act
Three plays of other times, and see
How the past truth of men is present fact:

Buckingham's changes of John Fletcher's *Chances;*
Then dumpy Ford, of the melancholy hat,
How in his tragedy of Calantha dances;
And Vanya, the dancing bear who tugs his chain too late.

So for a time we meet and share
The passions and humours of the heart,
To recognise our natures there.
And, at the evening's end, to part.

Until that time, however we may fare,
Our work, our hopes, our selves, are in your care.

Christopher Fry

After the three sessions of bows by the cast to all sides of the amphitheatre, a routine rigidly adhered to ever since, we were out in the foyer with the floodlights just begining to become effective in the gloaming to show the building in its beautiful starkness against a fading blue sky. The Board had agreed to have some sort of celebration in which all the populace could join and so take the theatre out of the select atmosphere some people might think it was in and bring it into the general community. So we had a a marching display by the Royal Sussex Regiment Band on the floodlight slopes of the park to the north of the theatre, and there was a tremendous crowd there already assembled as a result of the free invitations we had sent to every house in the city.

After this we had the finest firework display the city can remember and the theatre became established as part of the city and, I hoped, found a place in the hearts of the majority of the citizens. One other civic link forged that evening was the visit by most of the mayors of all other towns in Sussex, invited by the mayor of Chichester. After a reception in the famous Council Chamber they had gone in procession to the theatre preceded by the unique 'Mayors Moon' (a lantern) restored for this occasion and carried by the mace bearer as in the olden days when it was always used to light the mayor when he went visiting at night. Sir Laurence had viewed a heavy body of civic heads in the first night audience with dismay but to allay his fears we scattered them around and I know they were as light-hearted as any of the other members of the audience.

The only flaw that night was that the drinks for the cast, to have in the foyer immediately after the play, did not turn up. We never found out who omitted to give the order for them. The actors did not particularly mind when after the fireworks it was suddenly decided to entertain them instead in the theatre restaurant to a meal at about 11.30 when the public had gone. There was no time to issue passes so there were a number of gate-crashers. David Enders and John Glenn, with their Danish chef who loved a crisis, rose magnificently to the occasion and provided a meal for everyone.

It was a joyous occasion, with all my family around me, the Oliviers and their great friends the Mills family, with Hayley Mills, a new star in her own right, tasting the first fruits of public adoration. I felt self-conscious with some of the public still staring at us through the large glass windows even at that late hour, as though we were fish in an aquarium ; but the others were used to it. I thanked Sir Laurence and the cast in a short speech which was boisterously punctuated with remarks from the company. Sir Laurence affectionately thanked the actors for being a very happy company and helping him so loyally. We tried at times to see the

ITV broadcast of the opening but spirits were too high for anyone to listen quietly.

I lingered happily with my family gazing at the floodlit edifice, crisp in the summer night. The flags fluttered in a gentle breeze as they had done at the stone-laying ceremony just a year earlier and whilst we thought of many things I suddenly realised that time had begun to slow down for the first time that day. It seemed, that night, as though the park had accepted the building and the actors.

There had been a drama away from our theatre in London that very evening which was to affect us. That was the announcement in the evening papers, as we opened, that the Government had decided the National Theatre would after all go ahead and receive their backing. Much has been written, and there has been a good deal of surmising, about the timing of the announcement, with some saying that it was felt to be a good moment when there appeared to be a reawakening in theatres as shown by the way our theatre had caught the imagination and support of the public. I found it hard to believe it was any more than a coincidence, since Chichester must have seemed an obscure place, far away, to the politicians in Westminster.

I knew in my heart at that moment that Sir Laurence's time with us was to be limited, since it was taken for granted by everyone that he would be the Director of the National Theatre. In fact his appointment was not announced until August 3. Knowing that I should be anxious he telephoned me the night before the announcement to tell me of it, to assure me that his heart would still be in Chichester and that he would stay with us for a few more years.

It was interesting to remember his remarks to Lord Harewood in the *Tempo* interview in October, 1961. Lord Harewood asked, 'If you had the choice, the horrible choice I think, between deciding that there would be more Chichesters, more theatres of this sort and more festivals to go with them all over England or that there should be a National Theatre in London, which would you choose?' He replied :—

'Well, I think the more Chichesters there were in the South, in the Midlands, in the North, the more the vacuum will become so palpable, so painful in London, that I should think a National Theatre is bound to spring up to spare its own blushes. The need will be so poignant, the one will produce the other.'

Realities began the day after our opening with a rush for all the newspapers. There was a disappointing reaction from many of the critics. This was an extraordinary feature of the first years, not just occasioned by the quality of the plays. All three plays were praised for the standard of acting, but the main criticisms were of Sir Laurence's choice of plays and the use of our particular style of theatre. I was not surprised about the comments on the theatre, since I realised there was bound to be controversy and I welcomed it, because in this way this theatre would always be alive and interesting. Orthodoxy would not have survived, so we had gone out to specialise. The critics could hardly neglect or ignore a theatre such as this, but they probably travelled with a wish that it had been built nearer home.

Most of the older critics seemed to resent having to revise their views on proscenium stages. Many had spent a lifetime sitting in the best seats in front of a proscenium ; perhaps unmindful of those of the public who had to sit behind pillars, or at right angles to the stage, or high up and unable to see or hear properly. Now, presented with an open stage, they felt the draught of fresh air blowing across the future of the theatre, as in an open tourer compared with a limousine. Harold Hobson, of the Sunday Times and Christian Monitor, was an exception as he wrote many excellent articles on the virtues, and faults, of our stage and theatre. The years have mellowed the difficulty we had with the critics and we hear rather less of the oft repeated, and rather boring, phrases such as 'The wide open spaces of the Chichester stage'.

There was another element that hit us unexpectedly and which was nothing to do with Chichester. A new theatre built by an audience at that time might have been expected to receive encouragement and sympathy. Instead we met the effect of the announcement of the start of the National Theatre, which resulted in criticisms of Sir Laurence as a theatre director. The tenor of the criticism, though not harsh, was definitely pointed. The critics were trying to establish ascendency over him in order to instruct him regarding the choice of plays he should make for the National, if he was to gain their approval.

They reviewed his career and hoped he would not insist on the National having an amphitheatre stage like ours ; or if he wanted one, at least to have a proscenium stage theatre as well. I think our first year's criticisms would have been more favourable if it had not been for this underlying concern with the policies he might adopt for the National.

As I passed by the theatre on my way to the city next morning, after the opening, it seemed to me that we had created a huge monster lying in the Park, with hungry jaws waiting to be fed with people. It was not like starting a Society or a Club, I thought, which could be wrapped up one day and finished without loss of integrity or honour. Here was something to which I was bound for life. Directors and management could come and go as they, or we, pleased. Members of the Board could resign for good reasons, apologising for not being able to carry on, and would be forgotten, but if things went wrong I would most certainly have to exile myself from Sussex !

After the critics had their say we all anxiously watched the box office reports every day. Luckily the public had their own ideas about *The Chances* and bookings increased rapidly. To this day people still remember *The Chances* in detail as one of the best plays we produced. Obviously the use of the stage had not been fully mastered, and the excessive amount of movement was self conscious, but the play was beautifully dressed and a very gay choice for the opening.

The Broken Heart was not such a good choice, and it never really got off the ground. Huge, elaborate scenery, stretching from the stage right up to the roof, was a negation of everything this kind of theatre stood for. There were long corridors, reaching back and cut out of the scenery. These acted as holes to muffle the sound, emphasising the acoustic difficulty we were experiencing in the centre of the auditorium. This turned out to be due to a bouncing and intermixing of sound from two of the hexagon walls either side of the stage. This was simply corrected the next year by three slanting baffle boards each side of the stage. Acoustics in our theatre are good providing the scenery acts as a sounding board, in other words not too elaborate but of a flat dimension, and providing the actors speak clearly. Sybil Thorndike many times whispered her lines and even with her back to the audience could be heard everywhere. Many others are able to do the same without effort and this has been proved many times. *The Broken Heart* was a dreary play finely acted but even with Sir Laurence in it, the box office flagged. I shall never forget the wet and windy August Bank Holiday performance when the half full theatre was a most depressing sight.

Uncle Vanya restored the whole season and was a triumph in every way. It will always be known as 'the Chichester *Vanya*' and when we play over the record of the complete play it is heartrending to hear those voices once more. There could never be such a cast again, all playing roles of their own ages, all of them stars of the highest order. As time went on Sir Laurence told me how they had woven themselves into such a fantasy that they felt they were held together by gossamer threads. If one was slightly off colour the others felt it immediately and all would help and urge the play into a complete whole again. The critics were compelled to agree that this was an outstanding production. Sean Kenny's flat set worked wonders for the brilliant way in which the lighting was used and the few properties enhanced the acting. There were many all-night queues for this play.

I doubt whether any theatre has been visited by so many members of the Royal Family in such a short space of time. Princess Margaret and the Earl of Snowdon came during rehearsals, Princess Marina's first visit was on July 23 and Her Majesty the Queen and Prince Philip came to a gala performance for the Red Cross and St John on July 31. The next season the Queen Mother and Princess Margaret and Lord Snowdon came for charity galas.

On July 28 I paid another visit to Kensington Palace to arrange with Lady Pepys, sister to the Duke of Norfolk and Lady-in-Waiting to Princess Marina, about a visit to the theatre by Her Royal Highness. Princess Marina became one of our most beloved regular patrons in the years to come, always desiring to attend without ceremony so that she could fully enjoy the plays. I wonder if she ever knew how much the public loved her. When she died there were splendid leading articles in every newspaper, paying unique tributes to her, and I suspect she would have been surprised at their unanimous warmth. It is a pity so much is left unsaid about people while they are still with us. It must be especially difficult for Royalty to distinguish between prescribed politeness and what is real affection and appreciation.

One of the most amusing struggles between the professionals and lay people was the protocol of receiving distinguished visitors. The professionals are accustomed to the duty being imposed on the licensee of a commercial theatre, where the director or manager has leased the theatre and rents it from the landlord. In my opinion, a theatre such as ours, which is created, owned and run by the Board of a charitable Trust, should have one of the Board members to receive the guests in the first place and not the general manager. I find that this practice is followed by similar theatres. Generally Lord Bessborough and I, together with Sir Laurence, received the distinguished visitors and Sir Laurence always accepted this as correct. Not so the general managers, and I expect there will always be misunderstandings and friendly tussles over this in the years to come.

With Princess Marina coming to nearly all our productions, I gave up meeting her and Lady Pepys when I could see that this was a formality she did not require, but I always made a point that a member of the Trust was in the background, since I believe the Trust to be equally responsible with the police and management for the safety of Royal visitors.

On July 31 (during Goodwood race week) when her Majesty the Queen and Prince Philip came we had a day of near-tragedies. Just before the Royal party arrived a member of the audience, a man, walked clean through one of the glass partition windows of the foyer; luckily he was only slightly scratched. We hurriedly put a rail across all such windows next day. I had suggested some time before the visit that as all our seats looked exactly the same, and as the Queen would be in the middle of a long row with her party around her, it would save any doubt as to which seats were intended for Her Majesty and Prince Philip if they were covered for that night with red velvet. Unfortunately, the wardrobe department thought the seats had to be re-upholstered with the red velvet whereas I said just cover *over*. They did the upholstering perfectly to two spare seats and had expected it to a be simple matter to replace these for the existing ones. Alas, when they came to screw them in just before the performance, they found that all the seats are not the same size and so the newly upholstered ones would not fit. There was panic.

Seat holders had been specially asked to get to their seats well before the Royal party arrived, but the management had locked the inner doors while feverish efforts were being made inside to complete the two most important seats in the theatre. Pressure in the foyer was getting unbearable, and protests were beginning. I got into the auditorium by the way of the stage door to find out what was the trouble and argued that they would have to let the public in while the last screws were put back into the original seats and velvet hastily laid over. To make matters worse the foyer was still full when the Royal party arrived early from Arundel as the timekeeper's watch was found to be fast. We whispered the difficulty to the Duke of Norfolk and we all stooged outside making conversation with the Royal party until a guard of honour of Red Cross and St John cadets could form up. When they entered the auditorium, all was well with the seats, and no-one had noticed the cause of the delay. The National Anthem was sung that night by the Chichester Cathedral Choir, in their red cassocks, dramatically spotlighted on the balcony upstage.

It was a warm, stuffy night, and as we walked from the marquee where the Board had been introduced to Her Majesty during the interval, Prince Philip remarked on the need for air conditioning. I explained our difficulty over the awkward fire regulations. He suggested that we should lift the little top-knot in the roof and let some of the hot air out. We did this some time afterwards, and it did let out the pocket of very hot air that built up in the roof mainly from the stage lighting. At the same time it reduced somewhat the effectiveness of the air being drawn out under the stage, so it had to be regulated at times. The real trouble was that if the air in the Park was hot you were only drawing in hot air and the only answer would be refrigeration, which we could not afford at this time.

The next evening, at the Goodwood Ball at Arundel Castle, Prince Philip again told me how they had enjoyed *Uncle Vanya* and especially the style of the stage and the settings of the theatre. At the end of the performance, the Queen and Prince Philip were introduced, in the traditional manner, to all the members of the company and management on the stage as we watched from the auditorium.

From the time that the third play had been safely launched to the last night there were many occasions when the company were entertained, besides their own parties. There was the barbecue party around the swimming pool at Stansted where Lady Bessborough endeared herself to everyone by her genuine desire to see that each person there thoroughly enjoyed the evening. From the very beginning the whole idea of the theatre had caught the imagination of Mary Bessborough and besides helping financially at a critical moment she had joined in numerous discussions and helped with her artistic outlook. Her vivid sense of humour helped many an awkward moment.

We gave a party at our house to include all the stars and everyone working at the theatre. The gardens were illuminated, the theatre flag was spotlighted at the top of our flagpole, the band played for dancing, and altogether it was a night that many still remember.

On July 22 we had a delightful christening of the Oliviers' first child, Richard Kerr, in the Bishop's own private chapel. The Dean conducted the service and everyone was nervous that the solemnity of the ceremony would be spoilt by undue publicity, especially as the Bishop had been extremely kind to lend the chapel, a rare privilege. Only at the last minute did any of the reporters get knowledge of it. They chased the car for a quick photograph of the child, but it was all over in a minute and the Oliviers were soon well away from the Cathedral. We had a joyful buffet meal afterwards, with everyone from the theatre, at Woodend where the Oliviers were staying. They had announced another expectation, and so had Joan Greenwood as well as a member of the wardrobe department. It was a good thing the season lasted only until September 8 or else it would have been neccessary to replace them with understudies. We began to wonder whether in the future it would be better to have a maternity ward rather than the backstage additions.

We came to the last night all too soon and watched the last performance of *Uncle Vanya* with some nostalgia. To our surprise Sir Laurence broke his rule and spoke from the stage at the end. He paid a very warm tribute to Carol, myself and the family and went on to thank the people of Chichester and everyone who had been with him for the season. Later, in the foyer, there were presentations from the Board to the Oliviers of a dinner service, from the cast to them of a silver model of the theatre, and a silver cigarette box from the Society to us, organised by the ever-thought-ful Robertson-Ritchie, to commemorate the first season. I gave the theatre a silver loving-cup which was used in the traditional ceremony when the loving-cup is passed from person to person and on this occasion it began between us and the Oliviers.

Farewells were said and we returned home with the feeling of an anti-climax, only to find something to cheer us up . . . a bottle of champagne in gay ribbons hanging on our door with a letter of appreciation, for a wonderful season, from Mr Russell Purchase and his family, the wine merchants of Chichester since 1780. He wrote that it was the finest vintage champagne in his cellar and commanded us to drink it at lunch the following day. This we did, not in haste but with reverence for its quality and for the inspired thoughtfulness of a real friend.

Looking back, on this last night, I wondered what had made it all worthwhile. It would have been a great pity if it had never happened for it had added renown to Chichester for the future comparable with its past history. It had added an extra degree of prosperity to the city. It had fulfilled the hopes of those, like John English and Stephen Joseph, who had pioneered the thrust stage style of production and it helped at a critical time when, despite the wholesale destruction of theatres, there was a glimmering of revived interest in drama. It was becoming obvious that Sir Laurence would be forming the nucleus of the National Theatre company from among the actors he would gather around him during our next season. In any case our theatre was another building for actors to work in.

Certainly many people's lives had been altered and their outlook broadened. Lay people had learned from the theatre personalities that life could, with advantage, be more carefree. In reverse it was a new experience for many of the theatre people to work with professional and business people, unconnected with commercial theatres, and realise that many business axioms could, and should, be applied to running a theatre even in its artistic direction.

To me personally it would always remain an astounding fact that the theatre was there at all. It seemed unbelievable to see it there in the park. It was amazing how the right person came along at the right moment or said the right thing at the right time. It was also true that everyone who helped could claim that but for them it might never have happened. It was a slight shock that from the moment the theatre opened it suddenly changed from being my theatre, or the Board's theatre, to the public's theatre which they talked of possessively, criticizing it, or praising it, but nevertheless owning it. In terms of a game of 'snakes and ladders' there had been some exciting leaps up ladders and some sickening slides down snakes, but every time I saw the people, in their hundreds, looking excited and happy at the prospect of going to a show, or the sea of faces in the auditorium, I had a feeling of pride that we had all worked together to transform what otherwise would still have been an open space of parkland. The happiness it was giving was our reward.

So the first season was over and everyone departed : but ever lingering in our memories, and our thoughts for the future, there brooded the closing lines of *Uncle Vanya* so superbly rendered by Joan Plowright.

'. . . . and you and I, uncle, dear uncle, shall see a life that is bright, lovely, beautiful. We shall rejoice and look back at these troubles of ours with tenderness, with a smile and we shall rest.
I have faith, uncle ; I have fervent passionate faith.
We shall rest . . .'

We did *not* rest . . . but that is another story.

CHARLES HOWARD

...hester, a small Cathedral city, Roman in origin, predominantly Georgian. Population about ...oo, situated 60 miles south of London.

...w. Oaklands Park, a delightful 43-acre park just outside the northern city wall.

CHARLES HOWARD

WHY CHICHESTER?
Precedent and parallel

CHARLES HOWARD

Chichester city centre, with its celebrated Market Cross built about 1500 A.D., the Theatre Centre, and the Cathedral.

Above The old Chichester theatre in South Street (from a print dated 1805); and a view of East Street in the Sixties

D. L'OUVIBAR

Above left The amphitheatre at Epidaurus, Greece.

Above The Stratford (Ontario) Shakespeare Memorial Theatre.

Left A typical street in Stratford, Ontario.

There are many links between the theatres at Chichester and Stratford, Ontario. Among these are their park settings in small cities with similar populations and their open stage auditoriums.

'Trefusis', the Author's home in Chichester.

Tyrone Guthrie and Author. An alliance
is symbolized.

e families meet (*left to right*) Miss Guthrie, Sir Tyrone, Lady Judith, Carol and **David**.

CONCRETE VISION
The BBC make a film

Roy Rich interviews Sir Tyrone Guthrie in Oaklands Park.

CHARLES HOWARD

BBC camera team at 'Trefusis'

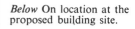

Below On location at the proposed building site.

With Victor Polley and
Tom Paterson at Stratford,
Ontario.

Scene from 'Coriolanus'.
A production at Stratford
in 1961.

Scene from 'Love's Labour
Lost', Stratford's 1961
production.

TAKING SHAPE
From fantasy to fact

Powell and Moya's brilliant first imaginative sketch of the Theatre in its park setting, and *below*, model. This clearly shows the consistency of the architect's vision with the final realization.

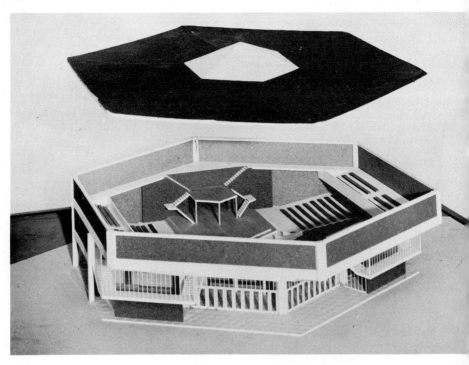

PORTSMOUTH EVENING NEWS

The original Theatre Committee meeting in the Elizabethan Room of the Old Punch House, Chichester. *Left to right*. C. Hodgetts, D. Goodman, D. Robertson-Ritchie, G. Marwood, F. Penfold, Cmdr. Bird, the Author, A. G. Draycott, Mrs Anstruther, C. L. Cox, P. Whitehead, D. J. Battersby, D. Palmer, P. A. Newstead.

Below are some of the original team. The other leading personalities are shown in the following pages

D. J. Battersby   P. Whitehead   Mrs H. Gestetner   Dr C. W. W. Read

Major G. F. Clarke-Jervoise   D. Goodman   W. Stirland   I. Wilson

The Very Rev. W. Hussey   G. Marwood   Barry Evershed-Martin   David Evershed-Martin

RAISING FUNDS
More of the first

The London Fund Raising Committee in session at Teddy Smith's flat in Bryanston Court. Teddy and Victor Behrens, joint chairmen.

The first Chichester Fund Raising Committee.
D. Hoare, N. Siviter, D. Robertson-Ritchie, A. Garrard, Comdr. Bird, Mrs Gibbons, Mrs Kitchen, Miss Montgomerie, Mrs Anstruther, Mrs Y. Rusbridg

Meeting of the London and Chichester Fund Raising Committees, at a cocktail party in the Old Punch House Chichester.
Major Clarke-Jervoise, Miss Rosita Barki, Mrs Kaden, A. T. Smith, Mrs Anstruthe the Author, Miss J. Evans, Mr and Mrs Robertson-Ritchie, Mrs Y. Rusbridge.

A few of the ladies who gave so much of their time to raising funds for the Theatre. They organized and staffed coffee mornings, exhibitions, bring-and-buy sales, and all kinds of social gatherings.

RAISING FUNDS
Social occasions

Lord Bessborough examines the gift of Crown Derby, presented to HRH Princess Alexandra. The set portrayed scenes from Shakespeare and the Festival Theatre.

CHICHESTER PHOTOGRAPHIC SERVICE

Back room boys. Organising the bungalow competition, J. D. Geddes, J. H. Vincent and Comdr. Bird.

GARLAND

Vivien Leigh at a fund-raising event in Pulborough.

Above HRH Princess Alexandra addresses the gathering.

Her Royal Highness lays the foundation stone, with Philip Powell assisting.

ohn Neville delivers Christopher Fry's 'Sonnet for the Oration'

BUILDING BEGINS
The first stone is laid

The Duke of Norfolk with HRH Princess Alexandra and Eric Banks, the Town Clerk.

With (*left to right*) Lord Bessborough, Teddy Smith, David Biart, Christopher Fry.

Above Awaiting presentation to HRH Princess Alexandra (*left to right*) P. Whitehead, The Hon. George Drew (High Commissioner for Canada) and Mrs Drew, Councillor W. Pope (Mayor) and Mrs Pope, John Rogerson (High Sheriff) and Mrs Rogerson, the Earl and Countess of Bessborough, the Lord Bishop of Chichester and Mrs Wilson, Carol, and W. Loveys (MP for Chichester).

The stone is lowered.

THE BUILDING GROWS
Mud, iron, and concrete

RICHARD HACKETT

CHARLES HOWARD

he early stages of construction. A remarkable example of modern building techniques.

CHARLES HOWARD

THE BUILDING GROWS
Form and texture

Behind the web of scaffolding the Theatre begins to take shape.

Sir Laurence addressing the workmen.

After the ceremony, with Russell Purchase and his wife talking to Carol and the Mayor and Mayoress, Sir Laurence Olivier and Alan Draycott in the foreground.

A critical moment. The last cantilever support is removed.

THE FINAL PHASE
The stage is set

Presentation of the maple stage from Canada by Victor Polley, the General Manager of the Stratford (Ontario) Theatre, and his wife.

Fitting the maple stage.

Sir Laurence treads the boards.

AEROFILMS AND AERO PICTORIAL LTD

The Theatre is complete. Below, Sir Laurence, as Director, waits to take possession.

EPOQUE LTD

THE THEATRE OPENS

Sir Laurence and Lady Olivier arriving at the Cathedral for the Theatre Evensong Service.

Above Leading civic dignitaries of West Sussex and Portsmouth, leaving the Restaurant for the opening performance.

Talking to the Duchess of Norfolk outside the foyer.

RODNEY SYMES

Above Dramatic lighting of the exterior lends magic to the uncompromising structure of the building, and sets the mood for the first night performance.

With Athene Seyler and Kathleen Harrison, 'A rose is a rose is a rose'.

THE FIRST SEASON
The Company

On the stage after a rehearsal of 'Uncle Vanya'. Assembled left, the administration and appeals staff.

At the Minerva Studios. Ivan Alderman and an assistant at work on the props and costumes.

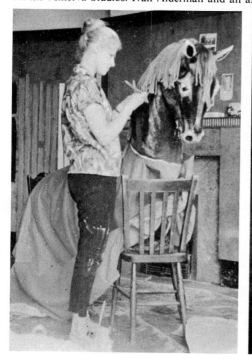

ANGUS MCBEAN

Centre the cast, and right the technical staff.

The lighting control panel.

The first book of the Theatre.

DAVID COLE

DAVID PAUL DESIGN GROUP

THE FIRST SEASON
The Plays

John Neville, Rosemary Harris and Keith Michell in 'The Chances' by John Fletcher.

'The Broken Heart' by John Ford.

ANGUS MCBEAN

'Uncle Vanya' by Anton Chekhov. Laurence Olivier, Rosemary Harris, Michael Redgrave and Joan Plowright.

Joan Plowright and Athene Seyler in 'The Chances'.

ANGUS MCBEAN

CHARLES HOWARD

'Come to Britain' Trophy awarded to the Chichester Festival Theatre Production Company Ltd. for enterprise in tourism during the year 1962 by the British Travel and Holidays Association.

The Author in 1956 as Mayor of Chichester with Her Majesty the Queen, Prince Philip, and Carol. The first official Sovereign's visit to Chichester for 50 years.

Below HRH Princess Margaret meets members of the Trust.

CHARLES HOWARD

Above The Queen Mother arrives for the Gala Performance of 'Love's Labour's Lost' by the Stratford (Ontario) Festival Company of Canada.

With the Author and Carol.

HRH Princess Alexandra talks to Sir John Clements.

DESIGN AND CONSTRUCTION

Reprinted from 'Architectural Design', Nov. 1962, by permission of the publishers.

SAM LAMBERT

Powell and Moya

Associate architect: Christopher Stevens

This theatre, seating 1,360, was built for a Chichester drama festival to take place in the summer months, starting in 1962. Building began in May 1961, when Princess Alexandra of Kent laid the foundation stone, and finished in May 1962.

The design, the first of its kind in Britain, is based on a recent movement in favour of the return to the character of the Greek and of the Elizabethan theatres, in which the audience virtually encompassed the players and where the stage was of a more simple nature than the modern proscenium stage. The detailed arrangement of the building was evolved in collaboration with Sir Tyrone Guthrie and Sir Laurence Olivier.

The theatre is sited at the edge of open park land, close to the centre of Chichester—the county town of West Sussex—about 65 miles from London. It is placed within a 'horseshoe' of mature elm trees and from the foyer there are fine views over the park. The theatre stands on the edge of a park with its main entrance from the Chichester/Midhurst road. At the south boundary of the site is 'Sloe Fair', which is a City Council car park for 500 cars. There are fine trees on the site, including some magnificent elms. These and all the other trees have been preserved. The hospital laundry will be screened from the theatre site by new planting.

Externally the aim has been to express as clearly as possible the internal design and planning of the building—the tiered auditorium encompassing the stage

is clearly seen showing its underside raised on supporting columns. The central area of the roof slopes more steeply than the rest, revealing to the observer on the ground that the building is indeed roofed over and not open to the sky.

By raising the auditorium off the ground, the whole of the space underneath it can be used—as an entrance foyer, dressing rooms, cloakrooms, etc. The supporting skeleton of the building is exposed and is of reinforced concrete cast on the site and bush hammered so that its aggregate is exposed. The infilling walls are of lightweight concrete planks painted dark brown. The stepped soffit of the auditorium is clearly shown. It is painted white and at night is lit from underneath, forming a brilliantly illuminated canopy to the building. The staircase windows are of wood planks painted white with narrow strips of glass between, giving inside a sense of enclosure and forming a transition between the glass-walled foyer and the windowless auditorium.

The audience is arranged on three sides of the stage which is placed at one apex of, and contained within, the hexagonal auditorium. The hexagon was chosen in preference to a circle for structural simplicity and economy, and because it is expected to give better acoustics.

The stage has a Canadian maple floor with traps, and the stage balcony, together with its staircases, is demountable. Across the back of the stage is a screen wall made of removable panels and designed so that

The main entrance with the stepped auditorium soffit projecting over it: painted white, it is lit from underneath at night to form a brilliantly illuminated canopy to the building. *Below* The supporting skeleton of the building is in situ reinforced concrete bush-hammered to expose the aggregate. The infilling walls are of light concrete planks.

DESIGN AND CONSTRUCTION

these may be rearranged to give exits in varying positions or be replaced by additional scenery.

There are nearly 1400 seats and the most distant are only 60ft. from the stage. Most of them have arms and seats upholstered in dark blue. Those in the back rows are of plywood, painted dark blue. The side galleries are not isolated from the rest of the auditorium, but form a continuation of the upper tiers. The lighting and stage control box has an uninterrupted view of the stage. The floor is covered with a dark olive green nylon carpet. The walls of the auditorium and the three tiers of the stage are painted in varying shades of warm grey. The foyer is generally white, with a floor of grey vinyl tiles. In the auditorium, production requirements, especially lighting, led to a neutral colour scheme. The roof is generally dark blue with supporting members in grey and black.

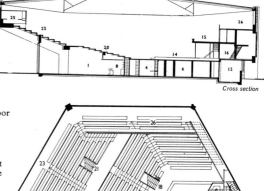

Cross section

The auditorium floor is stepped and made of pre-cast reinforced concrete, supported on reinforced concrete beams and columns which were cast in situ. The enclosing walls which are non-structural are of special insulating concrete planks. The roof has a clear span of 119ft. and its structural members are all visible from inside. It is supported on a 'cradle' of three tension members, each pre-stressed to 140 tons and each consisting of four 1¼in. diameter high tensile steel rods. These are anchored to the reinforced concrete frame at the top of the six corners of the auditorium and, by their pull on these corners, help carry the overhanging beams supporting the upper seating tiers. A ring beam of latticed steelwork is carried on the cradle and this ring beam in its turn supports the roof covering—a spider's web of light steel and timber joists, covered with wood-wool slabs which have an open textured finish in areas needing sound absorption and a smoother, harder finish where reflection is required. The roof is waterproofed with three layers of bituminous felt with a gravel finish.

Inside, the roof is painted dark blue and grey. Fresh air is drawn into the auditorium through fans which incorporate electric heaters. The air is drawn out through the open riser of the front step of the stage, along metal trunking to the ventilation plant room and thence to the outside air. The stage lighting and the main house lighting is suspended from a 'lighting bridge', a latticed steel structure and walkway which spans across the auditorium.

The building has been paid for by voluntary contributions from the public and the cost had to be kept extremely low. Little money was available for finishes and refinements. The building contract was for £95,064. During the course of building it was possible to incorporate improvements, due to the promoters' success in raising money, to a value of about £10,000. The lighting installation—largely production lighting—was not included in the building contract and cost about £18,000.

To keep initial building costs down, ancillaries normally provided with a theatre have been kept to a minimum. The temporary hutted accommodation for restaurant, administrative offices, scenery, etc., will, it is hoped, soon be replaced by permanent additions to the theatre which has been designed with this in mind.

The structural engineers were Charles Weiss & Partners, and the quantity surveyors were Davis Belfield & Everest.

The architects had the advice of John McLaren on the acoustics of the building, and of W. M. Campbell on tree care and landscaping.

The builders were Sir Robert McAlpine & Sons Ltd.

Auditorium floor

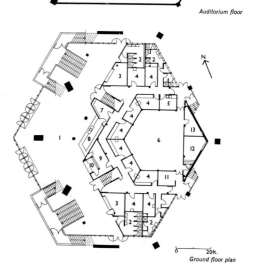

Ground floor plan

Above: cross-section and floor plans. The cross-section shows the cradle support to roof

Key: 1 main foyer 2 toilets 3 coats 4 dressing room 5 wardrobe 6 stage basement 7 bar store 8 bar 9 manager 10 box office 11 props 12 ventilating plant 13 switch room 14 stage 15 stage balcony 16 backstage 17 stairs from dressing rooms 18 stairs from foyer 19 front gangway 20 lower tiers 21 stairs from foyer below 22 upper tiers 23 upper gangway 24 main gangway 25 lighting and sound control boxes 26 gallery

The structural members of the 119ft. span roof are all visible from inside. There are the three tension members (four rods each) and a ring beam of latticed steelwork; the roof covering itself is a web of light steel and timber joists covered with wood-wool slabs. It is painted dark blue and grey inside.

The entrance foyer and bar, under the white painted soffit of the stepped auditorium. The floor is covered with grey vinyl tiles. *Right* One of the two staircase approaches to the balcony. On the left is the window wall of white-painted wood planks and strips of glass which give a sense of enclosure and form a transition between the glass-walled foyer and the windowless auditorium.

Opposite page Inside the spacious auditorium. The 1,360 seats are arranged on three sides of the stage, with galleries on each side continuous with the upper tiers at the back to preserve the unity of the audience and to ensure that no seat is further than 63 ft from the stage. The stage has a timber floor with traps, and demountable balcony and staircases.
Below left The landing half way up one of the two staircases to the auditorium. The staircase splits into two parts: one route ahead through the doors, the other lies in the opposite direction and leads to the balcony. *Below right* The lowest run of one of the carpeted staircases rising from the foyer. The bar is visible in the background.

MINERVA
A symbol for the Theatre

Many of our friends and supporters are familiar with the hexagonal motif used in all our publicity and displays. The shape, of course, relates to the plan of the Theatre, but until now we have been content to use an illustration of Chichester's Market Cross with the initials C.*f*.T.

It has become evident that we need an emblem with more dramatic flavour, more reference to the arts, and with a less localised appeal. This is a theatre for the South of England, and is not in any sense parochial. Yet we felt that since we are building the theatre in a part of England rich in tradition, and in a City whose antique origins are still in evidence, we ought to look for a symbol which links the past with the present, the universal with the particular.

Thus we chose Minerva, the Roman counterpart of Athene, goddess of the arts and sciences and associated with skill, wit and intelligence. Her war connections are perhaps best forgotten in this context!

Minerva (or Athene) is depicted in antiquity as a woman in armour; but with a decidedly masculine physique. She is shown with various symbols, among which the owl appears frequently, and this we liked for its legendary wisdom, and because, like the theatre, it is most active in the evening!

The appropriateness of our new emblem is, we feel, well established. The theatre itself, though as a building in concrete steel and glass, entirely of this Century, has obvious links with the Roman amphitheatre. Moreover, Chichester was an important Roman City, and we reproduce the celebrated Minerva Stone, discovered here in 1723.

Our interpretation of the goddess may not delight the pedants. The helmet, for example, has a decidedly Greek character, but it offered more decorative scope than the Roman varieties, and provides an allusion to the arena auditorium. In any event, Athene and Minerva are really only slightly differing aspects of the same deity.

If we have succeeded in creating a simple image which will help to identify us in the times to come, we shall be well satisfied.

DAVID PAUL DESIGN GROUP

A note by David Goodman reprinted from the Gala Programme of the Arundel Ball, 1961

CHARLES HOWARD

The Neptune and Minerva Stone discovered in 1723

Translation: To Neptune and Minerva this temple is dedicated on behalf of the safety of the Divine House, on the authority of Tiberius Claudius Cogidubnus, king and legate of Augustus in Britain, by the Gild of [?Ship-]wrights and its associate members from their own contributions, the site being presented by [Clem]ens, son of Pudentinus.

APPENDIX I

DR TYRONE GUTHRIE'S LECTURE AT THE ASSEMBLY ROOM, CHICHESTER MAY 3, 1960

This sort of theatre is a good idea. It seems to me that in this day and age we all look at drama going on in a rectangular frame and in two dimensions from breakfast, or way before breakfast and . . . right through till long after bedtime; virtually from cradle to grave so that there is no novelty in that kind of thing. The theatre now begins to be a sort of imitation of the 'telly'. It is a bigger 'telly' in colour but still the sort of theatre which takes place inside the frame is a two-dimensional carry-on, and as such suffers a cruel disadvantage.

I think it is time and circumstances which are compelling the theatre to come out again into the audience as it was until the restoration of Charles II in 1660. Before that, nobody ever thought of looking at plays behind a frame — that only came into being because, by the middle of the 17th century, the whole of Europe was being swept by what may be likened to a prairie fire just as strong and taking as the 'telly' — the prairie fire of the Italian opera or musical works. And they were placed in a frame for very good and sufficient reasons . . . the point I am trying to make is that the retreat of the theatre behind a frame, behind a curtain, behind the symbolic barrier of fire, behind the no less symbolic barrier of an orchestra and all the many symbolisms which put the players out of relation with the public, makes this side of the platform one thing, that side of the platform another thing. These two separate elements do not blend into one social and artistic mind. Those days, I think, are rapidly drawing to an end.

129

I am not saying for one moment — do not misunderstand me — that plays will cease in the near future to be played in proscenium theatres; of course they won't, nor am I saying that the kind of theatre they propose to build here is suitable for any or every kind of play; it is not . . . because all of us theatre people, including the authors, are tired of realism. We see that realism can go no further; in regard to realism we are in the same position as painters were when photography came in. When photographs could be taken, obviously the point of the portrait was that it should no longer be like the sitter. If you wanted a pure likeness you went to the photographer. Then the portrait became the element of comment, and became infinitely more important than the mere fact of likeness. So in the theatre; the movie, the television, these can provide photographs of things that are in a sense far more lifelike, they are not necessarily more life-giving; they are not necessarily more full of life, but they are a closer imitation of life. Therefore, the theatre must seek to do other things, not to be just life-like; it is not enough to go to a play and be satisfied and say, 'It is just exactly, it *was* Aunt Mabel,' because 'telly' has become far more like Aunt Mabel. . .

I am saying that the sort of theatre it is proposed to build here is suitable for plays written before 1660 and suitable for most of the forward-looking plays of the present day, but unsuitable for most of the plays between 1660 and the present day. Totally unsuitable for, let us say, Sheridan, Wilde or Goldsmith, or for Somerset Maugham. Not totally unsuitable for most of Ibsen where the poetical element is much more important than the realistic. Not unsuitable for the more important and greater works of Shaw; *Heartbreak House*, for instance, or *St. Joan* would be fine on such a stage as it is proposed to build here; *You Never Can Tell* would not, since that was a strictly realistic comedy, and as such would be far better inside a proscenium.

Now, you may say, 'Why build a theatre which is not suitable for any and every play?' The answer is another question: 'How to build a theatre which is suitable for any and every play'. Just as an all-purpose hall is a no-purpose hall, which is not very good for doing plays, not very good for concerts, is not very good for the Badminton Club, and not very good for the Church bazaar, so an all-purpose theatre is not a thing you can build. A play should be suitably presented in a theatre which offers the facilities which the author had in mind when he wrote it — that is my opinion. . .

Now why does one think that a theatre with a stage jutting out into the audience is better than the traditional thing, which for brevity let us describe as a Victorian opera house? First of all, because it does not offer any realistic scenic possibilities. That, I think, is vitally important in Shakespeare for various reasons. In most of Shakespeare's plays the scene changes very frequently ; let me take the instance of *Twelfth Night*. The scene changes seven times in the first five minutes of the play, or perhaps it is five times in the first seven minutes . . . There is no possible way of doing that in the twinkling of an eye, and the nearer you get to a twinkling of an eye the more obtrusive the scene changes become, because the audience stops listening to the text, and says : 'Wasn't that just amazing the way they changed the scene?' In a twinkling your eye sees them bundled from the Coast of Bohemia to Count Orsino's Palace, and they miss two or three important lines of the text, whereas if they come into the theatre and the scene is there, and the stage is there with certain architectural practicalities — a staircase, maybe, a balcony maybe, or whatever it is — of such a kind patently and obviously unchangeable, as permanently part of the building as those windows or these alcoves in this building, then people know at a glance that this scene is not pretending to be something it is not. It is simply a background to the players ; it is a piece of machinery. If somebody climbs up into that niche and somebody else speaks up to them from below, and the text makes it perfectly clear that one is on the ground and the other is at the first floor window [the balcony], then the audience will accept that ; there is no problem. The point about Shakespeare is this : always, where it is important that you should know where the scene is taking place, unmistakable indications are given in the text. And when it is important that you should know precisely where you are in space, indications are given in the text in a kind of language which makes it, in my opinion, a great impertinence to endeavour to out-do the language.

When in *Macbeth*, for instance, Duncan comes and says,

'This castle hath a pleasant seat' and then procee ds to describe it in fifteen or twenty of the most celebrated lines of poetry in our language . . . about the temple-haunting martlet . . . a series of indications are given with a matchless terseness, musicality and selection of what is important. You learn . . . that birds nest there, that it is a very sweet, pleasant, old, evening place. Everything that you need to know to appreciate the scene and the irony of this lovely evening, this charming castle and the poor old man coming in to where he is going to be murdered, all that is set up in lines of pure magic. I don't think it is a very good idea then that somebody, and not Leonardo da Vinci, paints temple-haunting martlets rather roughly on canvas; indications of time and weather and that kind of thing are given roughly and often with very inadequate equipment by an electrician, and so on and so forth. Better to be as Shakespeare intended it to be done by the actor who says to the audience what they have to imagine and leave it at that . . . In *Henry V* the chorus comes on and says, 'Think that you see our horses do this, that and the other. Think that this wooden O is the wide fields of France, and so on and so forth.' That does it. You are told what to think, what to imagine, the background is built up for you in the words. And when it isn't, it couldn't matter less. Half the scenes of Shakespeare take place in totally unidentifiable localities. The books say, 'a courtyard in Venice,' 'the Castle of this,' 'a street in London' and all sorts of things, but in practically every case those are simply deductions by editors of the text and all very literal, but they give the idea that it is important that one should know it is here or there, but it is not.

His characters meet. It is important that A meets B and the exact time of day, or the locality, or the country, or if any further information is important it is in the text. The answer is there. The point is the actors have got to speak it out good and loud and clear and place it intelligently in the context so that it comes to the audience in a way that they can pick up and understand and simulate and assemble the picture for themselves. But if all that is *literally* provided, various disastrous consequences occur. Irving's Shakespeare at the Lyceum, which our grandparents so very much admired and unquestionably very rightly, for these were the brightest people of a very bright era. One of the things greatly admired was stage pictures ; they were beautiful and distinguished and a great advance on almost anything that had ever been done in the theatre before, but they were achieved at the expense of the plays on a sort of back and front principle. There would be in the course of the evening three or four full scenes — elaborate, careful archeological reconstructions of whatever might be supposed to be the locality. King Lear's palace, which I remember seeing a picture of, was a great northern thing with great solid round arches and two or three gigantic round pillars, and maybe during the course of the evening three other great built-up set pieces which were masterpieces of the stage carpenter and the scene painter's art. But while these masterpieces were being very noisily prepared with many a curse and many a loud blow of a hammer and a screech of ropes and all sorts of extraneous noises, small-part actors have to come out whilst my Lord Northumberland has to meet my Lord Westmorland and York on a space the width of a mantelpiece, with the stage shuddering and the curtain billowing like a blasted heath. Very often those scenes were being played against the fusillade of curses and 'to me, Bert' from back stage. Even so, there very often wasn't time to prepare the big built-up set pieces and the play would be broken up into an eighteenth or nineteenth century editorial arrangement of five acts. Nothing to do with Shakespeare at all ; that's all editorial and there would be long intervals when the audience would come out and say, 'Wasn't it wonderful and all too heavenly !' and the loud banging went on, and to compensate for the time thus spent the text would be butchered. Again and again and again Shaw, the greatest dramatic critic in our literature, takes Irving cruelly to pieces, he tears him to bits for his butchering of the text of Shakespeare in order to make a stage carpenter's holiday . . .

In a theatre of the design which Mr Powell here has prepared, there can be no realistic scenery ; there is no mechanism for presenting it ; the scene is of such a kind that when the audience comes in, they can see at once that nothing can be done. They are not going to get any realistic pictures. What the actors tell them is going to be the evidence on which they can construct the pictures for themselves. That is not to say that the productions can be so dull as not to be picturesque. I venture to think they can be more so, because the dresses can be as sumptuous as anyone can afford and a great deal can be done by way of spectacle merely by the grouping of the actors if there are some steps to give them height. They can carry flags and this, that and the other ; great carpets can be rolled and unrolled again, none of which takes any time, but it can all make a feast for the eye, quite suitably spectacular but not in a realistic way and not in a time-taking-up way.

Now to the next point. If the stage comes out and the audience goes around . . . one important thing happens. You are making a far more economical use of the cubic space at your disposal, far more than the ordinary arrangement . . . This is not theory, this is a proven fact ; it enables far more people to be nearer the actors. At the theatre where I work and for whose design I was certainly not responsible, except in some sort of advisory capacity like here, 2,000 people are accommodated and the furthest away are in the thirteenth row, that is to say in row M. You know in an ordinary concert hall . . . it is nothing to go back to row XX or YY and ZZ, well back, and in the sort of theatre in which Shakespeare is normally played and which for obvious reasons has to be a big theatre, as Shakespeare needs a lot of people and a lot of people means a lot of hats, shoes, tights, swords, doublets, daggers and salaries, and to provide all that you have to get a lot of people out front, so Shakespeare is habitually played in very big theatres of a traditional sort. That means that the people farthest away from the actors, back at the gallery and at the side, are looking at the actors as though they were looking across a ten-acre field, and the actors lay their ears back and belt it out good and loud and clear. Now lots of Shakespeare is not susceptible for belting out and it is because of this that there has got around the totally mistaken idea that there exists something called the Shakespearean tradition which means [*declaiming*] TO BE OR NOT TO BE and so on. . .

If the actors are forced, as they are in a big theatre, never to drop below a sort of *mezzo forte* you lose the whole build-up of the climax, the whole artifice of speech from whisper to yell, from slow to fast, from — as it were — violin colour to brass colour. To have to play in a large theatre robs the thing of half its power, because if I am constantly speaking loud then, if I speak very loud it's only a little louder, whereas if I can go from a whisper to a yell, then there really is something dynamic. The same thing with speed; the same thing precisely with the optical thing. In a big theatre everything has to be enormously broad.

If you can get all the people around and near without compelling enormous breadth, the problem is how to get the people close and yet have a large enough capacity to be able to put on something with a big cast and a lot of expensive accessories. The only possible way is to make a more economic use of the cubic space than the normal commercial theatre does.

Now the next point I am going to skate over very briefly because it is highly technical and almost impossible to illustrate here. It is the thing of choreography. If you are working in a frame and the audience are sitting all on one side, that is perfectly logical and right for grand opera where the actors have got to face the beat and be in close rapport with the conductor; they are almost compelled for reasons of vocal balance all to face the audience all the time. That does not work any longer in the theatre. For many years — I would say until the 1920's — there were rigid rules, and it was regarded as almost breaking a serious taboo if an actor turned his back on the audience. More than anything else the coming of the movies caused the development of the whole idea of choreography in depth because in the movies close-up you can go right in on the face and the other person's — the other important actor — has the back of his ear taken. This accustomed the public to realise that the back of the person's ear can be really expressive, and nowadays plays have moved in a much more circular way. It is customary for whole scenes to be played by actors with their backs to the audience. The pattern is more flexible and this works on this kind of stage. You have entrances all over the place, the audience is all around. There will be entrances from under the audience like in a football stadium. The actors can also come down the aisle, or in from the back, instead of all the time working on lines parallel to the footlights.

(The foregoing is extracted from Dr. Guthrie's lecture)

APPENDIX II

SERMON PREACHED BY
THE LORD BISHOP OF CHICHESTER
THE RIGHT REVEREND ROGER WILSON, D.D.
AT THE CHICHESTER FESTIVAL THEATRE
EVENSONG IN CHICHESTER CATHEDRAL
SUNDAY JUNE 3, 1962

As the day for the opening of the new theatre draws near, it is right for us to meet here, first to pay tribute to those to whose vision the project owes so much. The speed with which the hope —to many it seemed a forlorn hope — has been realised, has turned from a dream into reality, may mislead us into forgetting how much has gone into its conception. To the few it is a dream come true, though the further dream that this theatre may become rooted in the life of the community still awaits fulfilment. It has been made by the few — their vision, courage, generosity. It has been made for the many — for in its very design there is something symbolic, as if to say that here the stage, planted in the arena of the ordinary world, shall speak more directly to us where we are, and involve us in the action taking place on it.

We need make no excuse for bringing this theme into the centre of the Cathedral worship with its sense of timelessness. Drama has sprung from the soil of religion : for long it was a part of man's worship, and its noblest themes have been the very issues with which religion is concerned. The two have never been wholly apart : there are still religious themes in drama, and there is still drama in religion. But the reason for bringing them to-gether here is not that this theatre will be concerned with religious drama (though in part I hope that may prove possible) : it is that the whole of drama must be concerned with life.

'I am a man' said the old Latin playwright Terence, 'nothing that is human is alien to me.'

All man's life, indeed, is grist to the mill for the stage. It rejoices with them that rejoice, and weeps with them that weep. It ministers to that tragic sense of life which is not far from any of us, purging us with pity and horror at the spectacle of the grandeur and the misery of man. It laughs at man in his pretensions and his follies, it laughs with him in his escapades and confusions. It plays upon his romantic longings, it records the annals of ordinary every-day relationships in all their many aspects. And so it shall be here. It must be a place where great drama is presented greatly — great because it touches life — in all the variety of subject and garb. And it is our hope that these opening seasons will so establish a tradition that the theatre will come through the teething years to full maturity.

It will be, like this Cathedral, concerned with the human scene. Our day was once dubbed the century of the common man, and in many ways he is the beneficiary of all our knowledge. We do not want it to become a common age in standards of taste. We do not want to be condemned to a life of endless rows of little houses all alike, an endless supply of gadgets, an endless line of people all dressed alike and committed to the same routine occupation. We are in danger of making our age an age of mediocrity. It is not that men live badly, but they live poorly, superficially, with a lower level of consciousness than they should. If this is an affluent society it is not really rich, but second-hand, cheap, in its entertainment, in its activities, in the incessant round of sights and sounds which can fill the hours but leave men empty of heart. You can call that life if you wish ; yet men do not come alive through a multiplicity of things, but through a few, deeply experienced. What do they really need? To stop and see the beauty in familiar things, to be aware of other people as real, to know sympathy and compassion, to love and even hate, to feel deeply, to discover themselves in personal response to the outside world, to find the meaning and hope of life. We need these if we are to live, and ordinary human life hurries so fast that it rarely gets beneath the surface.

The angels keep their ancient places,
Turn but a stone and start a wing :
'Tis ye, 'tis your estrangéd faces
That miss the many-splendoured thing.

We need awakening : and therefore drama must be the handmaid
of life, sometimes relaxing the pressure, so that we may take
notice and enjoy, sometimes pricking us into consciousness, lest
we sleep. For all this we would offer this new theatre, in its new
conception. If God is the Creator of life, if Christ came to give
abundance of life, if the Holy Spirit is the Quickener of life,
then everything which heightens our sense of living and calls
forth from us a new response can be enlisted in the divine purpose.
Some who take part here will do so as believers, and be aware that
they can offer their skill and their integrity to God Himself. All
of you, as believers or not, will be sharing in a ministry to human
beings for their well-being and their growth, which God can use
and bless. For that we pray : yet here in this building, in which
artist and priest have been allied to make a glorious place, there is
something more. Lord Bertrand Russell, in his ninetieth birthday
celebrations in the Albert Hall, said, 'I have a very simple creed.
I believe that life and joy and beauty are better than dusty death.'
Brave words, spoken by a brave old man (especially as he does not
share the Christian hope). Yet whatever they choose, men do tread
the way to dusty death, and they will ask their questions about it.
No-one can handle the themes of human life, can watch or reproduce its deed and moods, its exits and entrances, without
being drawn to ask what it is about, and whether there is in it
any intrinsic hope. You can bring all the world on to the stage,
but you may soon be asking whether all the world *is* only a stage
— and all of us just players. If life has no meaning, nor will its
drama. This building may move us, it may even kindle some religious emotion and add some colour, but it has not been built
for that. It was not raised to some vague 'Lord of Life' : it was
built on a drama acted in real life, it was built to the Word of God
made Flesh, to God who, dare I say, comes on to the stage with us,
who in His nature as God shares with us our nature as flesh and
blood, our tears, our hopes, even our dusty death. He takes upon

Him manhood, humbling it in His humiliation, exalting it in His Ascension. We are to conceive Him here, like that great enigmatic figure on the tapestry at Coventry, filling the building and dominating it — the God who takes human nature and lifts it up with Him, and now overshadowing us all, calls us in our human lives to share His life and be made like unto Him. It is this God, and no human actor, that can give nobility and hope to the dealings of men. This old building must stand behind the newer one, this undertaking (like all others) must be begun, continued and ended in Him — so that for us and others after us there may be a blessing in it.

APPENDIX III

PLAYS AND PLAYERS 1962–1970

PLAY	AUTHOR	DIRECTOR	DESIGNER	LEADING PLAYERS
1962				
The Chances	John Fletcher	Laurence Olivier	Malcolm Pride	Rosemary Harris Kathleen Harrison Robert Lang Keith Michell John Neville Joan Plowright
The Broken Heart	John Ford	Laurence Olivier	Roger Furse	Fay Compton Joan Greenwood Keith Michell André Morell John Neville Laurence Olivier
Uncle Vanya	Anton Chekhov	Laurence Olivier	Sean Kenny	Lewis Casson Fay Compton Laurence Olivier Joan Plowright Michael Redgrave Sybil Thorndike
1963				
Saint Joan	Bernard Shaw	John Dexter	Michael Annals	Max Adrian Jeremy Brett Frank Finlay Dudley Foster Robert Lang Norman Rossington Robert Stephens
Uncle Vanya (as above)				
The Workhouse Donkey	John Arden	Stuart Burge	Roger Furse	Fay Compton Frank Finlay Dudley Foster Robert Lang Mary Miller Norman Rossington Robert Stephens

PLAY	AUTHOR	DIRECTOR	DESIGNER	LEADING PLAYERS	
1964					
The Royal Hunt of the Sun	Peter Shaffer	John Dexter & Desmond O'Donovan	Michael Annals	Colin Blakely Dan Meadon Michael Turner	Robert Lang Robert Stephens
The Dutch Courtesan	John Marston	William Gaskill & Piers Haggard	Annena Stubbs	Frank Finlay Joyce Redman Billie Whitelaw	Caroline John John Stride
Othello	William Shakespeare	John Dexter	Jocelyn Herbert	Martin Boddey Derek Jacobi Joyce Redman	Frank Finlay Laurence Olivier Maggie Smith
1965					
Armstrong's Last Goodnight	John Arden	John Dexter & William Gaskill	René Allio	Albert Finney Ian McKellen Robert Stephens	Geraldine McEwan Ronald Pickup Michael York
Trelawny of the 'Wells'	Arthur W. Pinero	Desmond O'Donovan	Alan Tagg	Graham Crowden Gerald James Louise Purnell	Doris Hare Edward Petherbridge Billie Whitelaw
Miss Julie	August Strindberg	Michael Elliott	Richard Negri	Albert Finney	Maggie Smith
Black Comedy	Peter Shaffer	John Dexter	Alan Tagg	Albert Finney Derek Jacobi	Doris Hare Louise Purnell

PLAY	AUTHOR	DIRECTOR	DESIGNER	LEADING PLAYERS
1966				
The Clandestine Marriage	George Colman & David Garrick	Desmond O'Donovan	Alan Tagg	Bill Fraser Margaret Rutherford Alastair Sim John Standing
The Fighting Cock	Jean Anouilh	Norman Marshall	Alan Tagg	Michael Aldridge Sarah Badel John Clements John Standing
The Cherry Orchard	Anton Chekhov	Lindsay Anderson	Alan Tagg	Sarah Badel Tom Courtenay Bill Fraser Celia Johnson. John Laurie Ray McAnally John Standing Zena Walker Hugh Williams
1967				
Macbeth	William Shakespeare	Michael Benthall	Alan Tagg	Michael Aldridge John Clements Tom Courtenay Margaret Johnston
The Farmer's Wife	Eden Phillpotts	John Clements	Peter Rice	Michael Aldridge Diana Churchill Bill Fraser Irene Handl
The Beaux' Stratagem	George Farquhar	William Chappell	Peter Rice	Fenella Fielding Bill Fraser Maureen O'Brien Anton Rodgers Prunella Scales John Standing
Heartbreak House	Bernard Shaw	John Clements	Peter Rice	Michael Aldridge Sarah Badel Carl Bernard David Bird Diana Churchill John Clements Bill Fraser Doris Hare Anton Rodgers Irene Worth
The Italian Straw Hat	Eugène Labiche & Marc-Michel	Peter Coe	Peter Rice	Michael Aldridge Sarah Badel Peter Egan Fenella Fielding Anton Rodgers

PLAY	AUTHOR	DIRECTOR	DESIGNER	LEADING PLAYERS
1968				
The Unknown Soldier and His Wife	Peter Ustinov	Peter Ustinov	Michael Warre	Mark Kingston Clive Revill Prunella Scales Peter Ustinov Simon Ward
The Cocktail Party	T. S. Eliot	Alec Guinness	Michael Warre	Eileen Atkins David Collings Hubert Gregg Alec Guinness Pauline Jameson Nan Monro
The Tempest	William Shakespeare	David Jones	Ralph Koltai	Michael Aldridge John Clements Gordon Gostelow Hubert Gregg Richard Kane Mark Kingston Clive Revill Simon Ward
The Skin of our Teeth	Thornton Wilder	Peter Coe	Michael Warre	Hubert Gregg Pauline Jameson Millicent Martin David Nettheim Maureen O'Brien Simon Ward
1969				
The Caucasian Chalk Circle	Bertolt Brecht	Peter Coe	Michael Knight	Michael Aldridge Harold Innocent Richard Kane Heather Sears Topol
The Magistrate	Arthur W. Pinero	John Clements	Carl Toms	Michael Aldridge Renée Asherson Carl Bernard John Clements Christopher Guinee Brian Hayes Richard Kane Patricia Routledge Alastair Sim

PLAY	AUTHOR	DIRECTOR	DESIGNER	LEADING PLAYERS
1969				
The Country Wife	William Wycherley	Robert Chetwyn	Hutchinson Scott	Keith Baxter Gordon Gostelow Hugh Paddick Patricia Routledge Maggie Smith
Antony and Cleopatra	William Shakespeare	Peter Dews	Carl Toms	Keith Baxter John Clements Gordon Gostelow Margaret Leighton Hugh Paddick
1970				
Peer Gynt	Henrik Ibsen	Peter Coe	Sean Kenny	Judith Arthy Sarah Badel Roy Dotrice William Hutt Beatrix Lehmann
Vivat! Vivat Regina!	Robert Bolt	Peter Dews	Carl Toms	Edward Atienza Eileen Atkins Archie Duncan Leonard Maguire Sarah Miles Charles Lloyd Pack Richard Pearson Edgar Wreford
Arms and the Man	Bernard Shaw	John Clements	Peter Rice	Judith Arthy Sarah Badel Margaret Courtenay Laurence Harvey Richard Kane Charles Lloyd Pack John Standing
The Alchemist	Ben Jonson	Peter Dews	Carl Toms	Edward Atienza James Booth Dora Bryan William Hutt Richard Kane John Standing

144